Up Before Dawn

Up Before Dawn

By

Edward Kent

Edited by

Susan Payetta

Published in Grenada by Sail Rock Publishing
sailrockpublishing@gmail.com

ISBN-978-976-95346-0-5

Design: Paria Publishing Co. Ltd.

Table of Contents

Morne Fendue, Kent family home at St. Patrick's, Grenada

Acknowledgement:

Although the author is unable to thank the people who assisted with the completion of this book, the editor would like to acknowledge their contributions. Thanks to the Kent family for their encouragement and generous support, particularly Diana Wright (née Kent) for her assistance with gathering photographs and information from the family archives. Thanks to Lisa Kent, Karen Knights, Pam Horosco and Sydney Jacobs, and especially to Beverley Steele, for her enthusiasm and expert guidance.

Susan Payetta

January 2011

Foreword: Craigston Beef

"Sky always gets the head," says Edward.

"And does he always keep you waiting this long?" I ask.

We are sorting through receipts, tallying the accounts for Craigston Beef Ltd.

Since climbing stairs has become too treacherous, Edward prefers to conduct business from the main floor of his home. Edward's desk has been relocated from his office downstairs and we are seated in the shade on the verandah.

Craigston's organic beef is prized for its quality. In the early 70s, Edward imported a purebred Santa Gertrudis bull from Texas, via St. Lucia. This animal was used to upgrade the existing mongrel stock on the island and was replaced by purebred Jamaica Red Poll bulls from Barbados, who were in turn replaced by an almost pure Charolais bull from Tobago, affectionately named Diamond. Diamond has sufficient Indian blood to make him and his progeny tick-free and today continues to graze on the estate, enjoying his retirement.

The paperwork is under constant threat of blowing away in the breeze, so a variety of heavy objects are employed as paperweights. I'm searching for Skylark Stafford's receipt and lift the brass bell that is holding down a handful of notes, accidentally summoning Faithlyn, Edward's longtime housekeeper.

"Sorry, false alarm!" I call out, but a moment later she cheerfully appears through the wide-open space of the double-door entrance to Craigston Estate.

"Yes, Mr. Kent."

"Thank you, Faithlyn," Edward says, adding quickly, while he has her attention, "Oh Faithlyn, will you bring Ms. Payetta a glass of juice, please."

The bell is heavy brass and inscribed; Matthew, Mark, Luke and John. Edward has accumulated many objects of sentimental value over the years, and a story to go with each of them. I love hearing them and he is always grateful for an appreciative audience. The ledger isn't balancing but I soon find my error by cross checking the receipts with our order list. There are many accounts outstanding for orders that have already been picked up or delivered, and as I check through these I realise there are more people receiving gifts, than have placed orders. When I report the final figure to Edward, he seems satisfied with the result, even though he has given away more than he has sold, and I return his bank deposit book to him. Now just as soon as Sky comes to collect the head, the freezer can be shut down.

A week ago when the freezer at Craigston went on the fritz, it was looking like the end of Craigston Beef. Edward was trying to decide if he should invest in a new freezer or give up the beef business for good, when the repairman reported he had resurrected it. With the old freezer repaired just in time for Christmas, when a lot of family and friends are expected to visit, Edward made the call to Michael Frank and they dispatched the bull. He decided that was to have been the last one.

Edward reached this decision when he realised he could no longer hold up his end of the bargain with his partner Michael Frank, who tends their cattle. Michael used to work for Edward at Craigston

Bay Ltd. before the pastureland and lime factory were sold to some businessmen from Grenada with big plans for real estate development. He tends the remainder of the herd for the new property owners who want to keep a few head of cattle around the estate for "ambiance." Edward's role in Craigston Beef is to take the orders, schedule pick-up and delivery and handle the paperwork. Michael does the butchering and packaging. Edward himself dispatches the bull with one shot to the head, and they split the profits.

But Edward's health was letting him down. In spite of daily eye-drops, advanced glaucoma was conquering the vision in his right eye, and he hadn't seen out of his left eye for the last eighty years or so. His hearing was poor but with a new hearing-aid Edward could communicate very well with the volume on his telephone cranked way up. After Christmas '09 Edward was slowly gaining his strength back following his return from Barbados where he underwent emergency brain surgery to relieve an edema, the result of a fall during recovery from heart disease. Handwriting was a painfully slow process, and while he awaited an appointment for surgery in Grenada to correct carpal-tunnel syndrome, he persevered with the help of a wrist brace, using his computer to stay in touch with family and friends by e-mail. His mind was as sharp as ever.

Aware of these ailments and admiring Edward's determination to overcome them, I volunteered to assist him with his end of the bargain, but also for purely selfish reasons. I was in it for the beef! He accepted my offer graciously, and assured me that I wouldn't have to get involved with the actual meat processing. What I didn't bargain for was what a great time we would have, and how it would lead to my involvement in another more important project; the memoirs and oral histories of Edward R. Kent.

During his recent convalescence, Edward became discouraged because he thought he would not be able to complete his memoirs. When I accepted his request to help him with this project, he became very enthusiastic, sometimes working feverishly to complete his "homework," and always looking forward to our weekly sessions. We both thoroughly enjoyed these sessions until the prostate cancer he had been successfully treated for a decade ago returned, and he no longer had the strength to continue.

During a brief visit to his bedside at Carriacou Health Services, I said, "Edward, we finished so much more than we set out to accomplish, but you've left me with a cliff-hanger!" On the recording from our last session, Edward's final remark was, "It was illegal to . . . " when we were interrupted by Ken Nachajko, Edward's friend and companion, who lives in the chapel on the estate. Ken had arrived to serve the drinks, as he usually did at six o'clock sharp. But it was 6:15 p.m. and we had lost track of the time again. I shut off the recorder with a promise to continue the story at our next session, which never took place.

Edward beckons me closer to his bed and to my surprise, picks up the story right where he left off, completing the tale of the Duke of Edinburgh's Study Conference, solving the mystery as to what it was illegal to do, and proving that he never lost his ability to see a job through to the end.

George Kent and Sons

Childhood
at Morne Fendue

There is, in the family archives, a picture of my father George, holding the head of a resigned and docile donkey on which three small boys are seated. There is Ian, the eldest, then Paul, then me (Teddy, the youngest). I try to determine whether I really remember this occasion. Perhaps I just visualise the scene.

I do clearly remember the occasion when they were pitching the road up by the big silk cotton tree near Rose Hill, at the base of which all sorts of jumbies dwelt. I was tailing along behind brother Paul, and his friends. The area must have been out of bounds as–though we were free to roam the fifteen acres that comprised Morne Fendue Estate–we were not allowed to leave the confines of the estate without Mother's permission . . . and Mother's, or *Mammy's* word was law. But the "steamroller" was compacting the macadam! which would have been equivalent to going to see the Concorde take off today.

As I recall the scene, a man came out of a small house and made a face at us. All ran for home, but my body went faster than my little legs could match, and I fell forward onto a sharp stone cutting my forehead quite badly. I do not recall how I got home, but I have a clear vision of being in the trap at the top of the gap with Betty beside me, reins in hand. I remember Dr. Roy Hughes (from whom I got my middle name) stitching the gash–without the aid of anaesthetic–and giving me a paradise plum to quell my bawling.

Mammy ruled the roost with a gentle dignity that discouraged contradiction or disobedience. I remember her lying on the big brass bed in the front room, known later as "Mother's Room." At six o'clock every morning a maid in starched cap and apron would bring her "tea" on a tray. I never thought at that time of the early start the maid must have made to light coals to boil water for the soft-boiled egg and tea to be presented at 6:00 a.m. If this sounds like a slow start, it didn't last long. The domestic staff had to be supervised and directed, though there was a set itinerary for maintaining the big house in pristine condition. There were set days for polishing furniture, brass and silver adornments. I think it was every Thursday that the stair rods were removed and polished. Certainly it was every Monday that a mountain of dirty clothes and linens were gathered, checked by whichever of my sisters was home and collected by Mrs. Phillips, who took it to the river, beat it on the stones, starched what was appropriate, ironed it all, packed it neatly on the big tray and carried it back on her head to be checked, and to receive a few shillings reward. I remember Agnes (an under maid) receiving 18 shillings a month. But then Daddy was paid but £200 per annum, so money was tight at all times.

Daddy's was a fairly set regime: rise from the big brass bed before 6:00 a.m. and repair to his room, then plunge into the metal bathtub, which was filled automatically each night by the overflow from the overhead galvanized iron tank that lived in the attic. Since a 4" water main from Mt. Reuil served the whole valley down to Sauteurs and beyond, pressure was low during the day and only built up to Morne Fendue at night. This made the storage of water for house and garden use essential. Daddy would have his breakfast at the dining room table, another soft-boiled egg (he never seemed to mind how cold it was) and two slices of toast, and then mount his horse and set off for Plains Estate. Except on every other Friday, when he would mount car or motorcycle to head for Simon Estate, the Grenville bank and "The Club."

Sometimes, during the holidays, I would trot along beside his horse as he rode to Plains, about a mile away, and frequently he would stop at the bottom of a track and call out, "Mary!"

"Yes, Mr. George!" was the reply, and a child would come running down to be given a letter from a relative abroad. All the parish mail was distributed from the Post Office in Sauteurs. Every afternoon at about 2:30 p.m. the yard boy set off for Sauteurs to buy fish and ice and to collect the mail. People had started following the Carriacouans example and emigrating to Aruba, Curacao, Maracaibo, etc. They addressed the homeward mail, "c/o Mr. George Kent, Morne Fendue." I recall an evening when the yard boy brought 72 letters and only two were for Daddy.

In retrospect, the routine at Morne Fendue seems almost dull, but on reflection I recall that there were often events to break the monotony of life. I never attended a formal school before I joined Birnam Preparatory School in London when I was thirteen. In early days I was taught by *Mish Bain,* our governess, but after Paul went off to the Grenada Boys' Secondary School in St. George's, Miss Bain vanished and I was taught by Mother, Marcelle and Betty (my sisters), Sheila MacEachrane (daughter of the Anglican priest), Mr. Charles (Principal of the Anglican Primary School in Sauteurs), Aunt Emmy Copland (who tried to teach me Latin) and cousin Muriel (who taught me algebra and geometry). To that end I rode a horse across the parish (about four miles) to Mt. Rodney twice a week. Sheila taught me on the back verandah of the Anglican rectory and Mr. Charles gave me private lessons before his school started at 10:00 a.m. It was unthinkable that George Kent's son should attend the primary school. Why Mother never sent me to GBSS, I know not. Perhaps she was saving the pennies as she was determined that I should have an English education (in spite of reduced circumstances) as both her and Daddy, and all my siblings, had.

Church on a Sunday morning was a must. There was never any question about it. All the family dressed up in their Sunday best and were driven to church by Daddy. Our rented pew was but three pews back from the front on the left side of the central aisle, so immediately below the pulpit and not well positioned for sleeping during the sermon. All the gentry had their allotted pews; the names were held in little brass holders screwed to the shelves, and woe betide the stranger who trespassed. But the most galling thing about being dressed up in stuffy clothes for church–at one time I was required to wear a sailor-suit with a big blue collar and white topee–was the inordinate amount of time the grownups spent standing around the church yard gossipping after the service was over.

This was very irksome to a small boy, who wanted to get home, take off his shoes and those stuffy clothes and climb a tree or fly a kite, though I'm not sure that those pursuits were permitted on Sundays. Certainly I know that no games or jazz were allowed. About as much as was allowed was to compete to see who could catch the most flowers floating down from the big cedar trees in the front. If it was raining, we stood around the upright piano with Mother playing, and sang hymns and Gilbert & Sullivan lustily.

The history of the cedar trees is worth mentioning. Daddy told me that when Morne Fendue was being built (c.1907), his godfather, Mr. Ruggles Ferguson, rode over to see the house abuilding. As they stood on the front step, Daddy told him that he proposed cutting down the eight cedar trees that stood on the rise beyond "the circle." Mr. Ferguson responded, "George! You could put a man with an axe and cut down those trees in a few hours, but you couldn't replace them in a hundred years!" Daddy excavated off to the side for a tennis court that was never built, the trees stood for many years and the area was known as "under the trees." They were severely mauled by Hurricane Janet in 1955 and the ravages of old age and termites have accounted for all but one.

One Sunday evening when I was about nine or ten, my parents had gone off to dinner at Government House and my brother Paul and a friend named Willie McNeilly and I were ragging around downstairs in the house at Morne Fendue. My sister Marcelle, who was preparing to be escorted to a cinema in Grenville (big deal!) put her head over the banister and yelled down at us, "Will you boys be quiet?!" So we went out under the trees. But on the way out, Willie grabbed a hand towel from the hand basin in my father's office, wet it, and he flicked this at me and I ducked. I ducked right into it. It wrapped itself around my head and the tip caught my eye and pulled it to the side.

I can remember being back in Morne Fendue lying on the couch and looking up at the electric light which was blurred. I think I probably went to sleep, and the next morning this was reported to my parents. They called in Dr. Copland, (an Edinburgh man, don't you know!) the local GP. He was putting drops in my eye that burnt terribly, and I had to be held down, more or less. Mother insisted on sending me to the hospital in St. George's for a couple of weeks where they put drops in my eye, which did not burn. I was having a great time because the nurses would apply to the steward for extra ice, and with this ice they would churn ice cream. So I would get ice cream every other day, and they were all very kind to me but there was no progress. So then my mother took me to Barbados to Doctor St. John, who was the leading ophthalmologist. He treated me for a couple of weeks and pronounced, "detached retina." Nothing could be done in those days so I just learned to live with it.

As Paul was three years to the day older than I, and our friends Roy Copland and Claude MacEachcrane went off with him to school in St. George's, I was left much on my own during the terms. The void was filled by two lovely dogs that became, in turn, my companions and friends. Dale was the first. I remember Daddy bringing him home from Grenville, a present from Mr. Walter De Gale. Dale was a bull terrier of great personality and we loved each other dearly. Shortly after he died, I got Terry, who died of a broken heart when I was sent off to England.

Fulfilling Mother's wishes for me to have a proper English education, suffice it to say that when I sat the entrance exam to Emmanuel School in London (where Paul was already a pupil) the English master told Paul that I had done the best English test that he had ever seen. I take no particular credit for that. As we lived in what was considered at the time to be an outpost of the empire, Mother, in particular, rammed English grammar down our throats, whether we wanted to learn it or not. By contrast, English children were not taught English grammar.

An unintended part of my early education happened one evening when Daddy was driving us home in the Pontiac (with a cloth roof and open sides). Near the bottom of the gap (only later did some try to dignify it by calling it the driveway) we encountered a drunk man swaying in the middle of the road. Daddy tried to pass on the left but the man staggered that way. He swung to the right and the man followed. As we did eventually get past, I called out, "Get out of the way, you stupid old man!" and got roundly cursed by him. I cried, "Daddy! Did you hear what he called me?" and my father said,

"Teddy! If you had not spoken to him that way, he would not have spoken to you that way!" That was a salutary lesson that has stayed with me for the rest of my life . . . and stood me in good stead.

Daddy was an excellent sportsman, excelling in many different disciplines. After leaving school in England he played rugby football for the London club, Croydon, and had a collection of newspaper cuttings about his performances for that club. The last one read, "Croydon is losing the services of G. Kent, who is going out to the West Indies to manage his father's plantations." I was told by a contemporary of his that if he had not left England he would have played rugger for England. On returning to the West Indies he captained Grenadian teams in football and cricket. He and his brother-in-law, George Gentle, were Men's Doubles Tennis Champions of Grenada for twelve years. During this time they went to Trinidad and beat the Trinidadians.

Daddy showed me the spot at Clydebank, St. Patrick's where the first tennis court in Grenada was reputedly built; and the spot at Mt. Craven, St. Patrick's where there was a court. The tennis players of St. Patrick's met regularly on Wednesday and Saturday afternoons to play. There was no club house but Uncle David Gill would travel with a small wicker basket in which whiskey and soda-water bottles were packed, and a flask of ice, when it was available. After a set he would disappear behind the water-wheel, trailed by one or more invited gentlemen. The ladies were never invited. I was never sure to whom this tennis court (in the middle of nowhere) belonged. By the time I returned to Grenada in late 1939, the tennis had been discontinued. The other tennis courts in the parish were at Trevellan, Mt. Rich and Samaritan. I was never encouraged to play–children were to be seen but not heard–but was quite happy to be "ball boy" and keep the players supplied.

St. Patrick's at that time was a closely knit parish. Being rather remote from St. George's and even St. Andrew's, the intelligentsia of St. Patrick's mixed freely and did not keep aloof in cliques of rich and poor, white and brown, young and old. When there was a picnic at

Levera, everyone of the "upper class" was invited. Being a member of the upper class did not necessarily mean being wealthy; the rich provided the bigger picnic hampers, while the poor brought what they could afford–sometimes only a tin to carry home some of the leftovers. Those who had cars or traps took those who had no such luxuries. The young learnt to mix freely with the elderly and to treat them with proper respect. St. Patrick's was noted for its hospitality and people from St. George's were honoured to receive an invitation to one of the Great Houses for a weekend.

Those were idyllic days at Morne Fendue and today I find myself humming, "Those were the days my friend, I thought they'd never end . . ." This idyllic scene would be interrupted by the departure of members, such as when my sisters Jocelyn and Marcelle went off to school in England, followed a few years later by Betty and Gwen, or Gwyneth as we sometimes called her, to her chagrin. I do not remember them going but I remember Marcelle being at Morne Fendue (she taught me for a while before she returned to England) and I remember Betty and Gwen returning. Gwen played the cello. How embarrassed she was when our parents were entertaining and Marcelle was called upon to sing, and Gwen to play.

The family migrated to Green Island for the month of August each year. What fun that was! The whole family–including children and dogs and "domestics"–together with camp beds and bags of provisions were driven to Levera Beach where David Swan and his minions would be waiting with boats in the surf. The timing was very important as the tide swept between the islands at three to four knots per hour and arrival an hour late could result in a six-hour wait until the tide changed. The month on Green Island was always a treasured event. The sea was at hand for easy fishing and swimming in, there were always resident visitors whose presence seemed to break any monotony, and others who would come up for the day or the weekend. But it was in 1927 that Daddy bought the Carriacou properties and the annual trek was to Craigston. The operation was similar to that when we went to Green Island, but now a sloop would be chartered from Carriacou and the whole family, plus appendages, would embark from Sauteurs and sail off to Carriacou. It was all-hands-on-deck, as there was no passenger accommodation and often down below would reek of bilge-water and decaying fish.

Fun though Green Island was, the expedition to Carriacou was even more exciting. As the sloop had no engine, we were at the mercy of tide and wind, and the trip (tho' but 25 miles) could take eight hours. No matter, it was such an exciting adventure that the time seemed to pass quickly. We set sail in the early morning and got to the Carriacou jetty in daylight. We were rowed to the jetty–the vessel never braced–and piled into the Model A Ford Truck, driven by Sandow Glean on the white sand roads, up to Craigston. The Carriacou of 1927 was a far cry from the Carriacou of today. Apart from some lime trees at Craigston, Grand Bay, Dumfries and Lauriston, the crops grown were cotton, corn and peas, and groundnuts in the Belmont/Bellevue South areas, all of which required full sunlight, so there were few trees. Unlike Grenada, with its cocoa, nutmeg, breadfruit and other trees, the whole landscape was open for miles.

The month spent on Carriacou was always exciting. Usually a friend or friends were invited for at least a portion of the time. There were horses to ride, the sea to swim in, and catapults to be made to stalk the doves that abounded.

Since the boiler that supplied steam to the still that produced lime oil was fuelled by wood, some 200 to 300 cords of firewood were purchased each year from the owner of Anse La Roche Estate, and in August there would be an enormous pile of firewood in the lower part of the factory and in the yard outside. As I was not a proficient swimmer, this pile provided an endless supply of logs which I could straddle and cling to, and try to keep up with the bigger boys who swam out until they could see Craigston House over the profusion of manchineel trees that lined Craigston Beach.

I can still remember the feeling of stability and security that surrounded me in those days. The expeditions were few and far between and even visits to St. George's were rare, but I was confident that were I dropped anywhere on Grenada or Carriacou I would just announce, "I'm George Kent's son!" and someone would take me home. I perhaps did not appreciate this feeling of security properly until the first day I walked down an English street and said, "Good morning, sir," to an Englishman in bowler hat and pin-striped suit who turned around and looked me up and down as though enquiring when I had come down from the trees.

The incumbents at Craigston were Sandow Glean, the engineer, and Fedner Archer, a nephew of Tom Archer, who was the manager. They lived at Craigston House when the family was not in residence. When it was, they retired to the small room at the end of the back verandah. There were three horses in the stable and the groom, Whitaker, who would provide saddled horses for expeditions

There were but three bedrooms so, with Sandow and Fedner occupying one, the other two became dormitories for boys and girls. With the limited beds, cots, hammocks and mattresses placed on the floor were brought into use. But it was so different to Grenada that we felt that it was like going on safari. Generally my sisters would bring one or two girlfriends, and Paul and I would bring a friend and everybody had great fun.

At the back, detached from the main house, were the kitchen and servants' room. In the kitchen was the dover stove; a wood fired iron stove that was heated by a supply of dry wood brought in from the surrounding fields by the yard boy. He tended the three or four cows; milked them every morning, tied them out and brought them in for water at noon every day. He also fed the pigs, pumped water for the house and did whatever chores were assigned to him. There was very little garden to care for. Later Mother imported a separator that extracted the cream from the milk. Added to guava or cherry stew, this made a really delicious dessert, but the majority of the cream was converted into equally delicious butter. Mother even sold small quantities of butter to people in Grenada, but that was later–in the '40s.

But all good things come to an end. In 1930 Paul was sent off to school in England and early in 1933 I heard ominous remarks about "Teddy going to England." I was but twelve so nobody thought to ask my opinion about the matter. It seemed it followed like night, the day, that Teddy should follow the example of his siblings and go off to school in England. It was true that Jocelyn and Paul were there, and Marcelle was in Paris, but I had a heavy heart at the thought of leaving the warmth and comfort of my parents and the entourage at Morne Fendue. Worst of all was leaving my dog, Terry. He was a bull terrier of superior intelligence and we were almost inseparable. He was strictly forbidden to come upstairs but as soon as the front door was opened in the morning, Bruno (Daddy's dog, who was fourteen and had never been allowed upstairs) would dash to the bottom step and try to prevent Terry from coming up. When he succeeded in outwitting Bruno, Terry would be up and on my bed in a flash, much to the displeasure of Mother, who objected strenuously. Terry's face got longer and longer as he seemed to sense that I was going away.

In those days it was never certain that the Pontiac would start, so for a long expedition like St. George's, Daddy would get the car out early and park it at the top of the gap. Stones were put in front of the wheels to ensure that it did not take off unbidden. When it was time to leave, having said goodbye to the staff, I ran through the house looking for Terry to say goodbye. I found him sitting like a sphinx on the wall alongside the car. He was just staring down the gap and would not respond to my call. I threw my arms around him and hugged and kissed him but he sat as though made of stone. As we drove off, I looked back and he sat there with a reproachful look. A few months later he was dead, and no one could tell me of what he died. But I thought I knew. . . .

In St. George's I was introduced to Rev. Hatch and family, in whose care I was to travel to England onboard the *SS Ingoma*, of the Harrison Line. It was with heavy heart that I said goodbye to my family and climbed aboard to be rowed out to the *Ingoma*. I do not pretend to remember, but I think it would be safe to say that I cried myself to sleep that night. After an overnight trip we put into St. Lucia for coal, then another overnight took us to Barbados. There I went to a family of Inness' (friends of Mother's) for the day, while the ship was loaded with bags of sugar and baskets of coal. I cannot remember anything pleasurable about that trip. I felt very much the odd man out and got no comfort when the white cliffs of Dover were pointed out to me through the early morning mist some ten days later.

The trip up the Thames was even more discouraging. The river looked oily and polluted and the buildings were black with grime. My heart sank even more when the passengers started disembarking and there was no sign of my sister Jocelyn and brother-in-law Teddy Forshaw, who were to meet me. My guardians said goodbye and only the purser, who was counting up his gratuities, was visible on the upper decks. I felt more alone than ever. Eventually, when all hope was fading, Jocelyn and Teddy arrived in a sporty car with the top down. Fortunately, it was a bright and sunny day but when Teddy parked outside a tall office building in the city and left us to bake in the hot sun, I was even more unhappy. Eventually he emerged and drove us down to Birnam Preparatory School and my heart rose several notches as the gardens were beautiful, with roses and other flowers I could not identify. I was welcomed by the Brennans, who took me in and showed me to my room (shared with Paul) at the top of the house.

My school portrait

English
Education

Going to live with the Brennans was a really traumatic experience for me. It was the first time I had lived away from home and, whilst Mrs. Brennan was kind and understanding, Mr. Brennan, the proprietor and headmaster of Birnam Preparatory School was severe. Paul had been their 3rd pupil and had lived with them for some three or four years, even after he transferred his schooling to Emmanuel School at Clapham Junction. I was their 30th pupil as the school had expanded rapidly.

When I stopped boarding with the Brennans, I think they had sixty-three pupils. The Brennans had one child, an eight-year-old daughter Bridget, who was idolized by her father and who was rather unpopular as she was constantly running to her father with tales that brought retribution to the pupils. The only other resident was a German girl, Hildegarde, who was supposed to be a sort of governess to Bridget.

It was a rude awakening to the discipline of an English household. "Shut the door! Turn the handle to the full extent before pushing so that the lock doesn't click; If you need someone upstairs, you don't shout–you go upstairs and find them; Take off your shoes as you enter the house; Don't speak unless you're spoken to."

For the two winters I spent with the Brennans I had terrible catarrh that caused me to cough a lot and earn the ire of Mr. Brennan, who never failed to berate me at breakfast and tell me that I had kept the whole house awake all night. So, every Wednesday afternoon (during the winter) when we had half-day school, I would sit in Dr. Rose's clinic and soon had drops to put in my nostrils three times a day, pills to take twice a day, and Friar's Balsam to inhale twice a day. I was even sent to a Harley Street specialist, all to no avail. At night I would bury my head in a pillow and try to smother the cough, or even sip very cold water in an attempt to ward off a cough, but nothing worked.

The school was a conventional house with a large room at ground-level that was the senior classroom. The asphalted playground ran from the outer door to a wooden classroom that had been built to accommodate the additional pupils as the number grew.

Years later I came across a letter in Mother's trunk which lived under the window in her room. In this letter Mr. Brennan wrote, "Occasionally in one's teaching life, one comes across a pupil whom it is a pleasure to teach. Such a one is Edward," but there was no hint of this in his conduct toward me. Only after I left and returned to visit did he get expansive and say, "Edward! You know that the door is always open and you're always welcome!"

I have a vague recollection of being taught songs like, "Land of Hope and Glory" and "The Frog He Would A-Wooing Go," but little else. Soon I was promoted to the senior classroom, adjoining the house and then Tom Kilby joined. Tom was a gangling youth of sixteen and over 6' tall. He had been pushed down some stone stairs and injured when he was a pupil at Wimbledon College; had been sent off for a year to his grandmother's farm in Shropshire and resumed his schooling at BPS in September 1933. We became fast friends. His mother became my English-mother and his home my English-home.

During this time my brother Paul attended Emmanuel Public School at Clapham Junction but continued to board at the Brennans.' He commuted on foot and by train to Clapham, which was reputed to be the biggest railroad junction in the world. At this time my sister Jocelyn and her husband Teddy Forshaw lived in a bungalow at Worcester Park; a new development a few miles out off the newly-built Kingston by-pass (considered a superhighway at the time). I remember visiting them there but I do not think I ever stayed there. Not long after, they moved into a three-storey house, No. 99 Kingston Road. This was within half-a-mile of BPS but I did not see much of them except during the holidays, when I sometimes stayed with them. Their son Michael is ten years younger than I, so if I was thirteen he was only three. They had musical pretensions and often held soirées with musicians from various orchestras participating while I sang (I had quite a good tenor voice) or Jocelyn played the violin. It was an anomaly that, though Jocelyn had earned a diploma in piano from The Royal Academy, she dropped it and took up the violin. It was fashionable on these occasions to drink Chianti and, as these gatherings often continued until quite late, I often found myself having to get breakfast for Michael and I; then *Hoover*; then go to the shops to buy something for lunch; peel potatoes, etc. Jocelyn would take over around noon.

Sometimes, in the summer, my sister Marcelle would come over from Paris, even bringing her son, Jean-Michel on one or more occasions so that he could learn English. These were always brighter interludes. She would darn my smalls and generally get my clothes into better shape and manage an expedition of entertainment. Otherwise, life was pretty drab and I was very glad of the Kilby's "open house" to me.

Tom and I, along with two other boys, Donald Begg and Fred Martin, were the senior boys in the school and were soon calling ourselves "The Four Musketeers" as we often went on exploits together. It was during this period that Tom introduced me to the joys of cycling. With the help of the christening fund that Mother had established, I bought a Raleigh Sports for £4.19.6p. The first time we cycled ten miles together, I had to write immediately to tell my parents. The distance from Sauteurs to Grenville was eight miles and this was further! The distances grew longer and longer until we were regularly riding out to Maidenhead of a Saturday afternoon with a banana, an orange, and a bottle of KiaOra orange squash. With pocket money of 1s per week, we couldn't afford more. We even cycled down to Brighton and back, one Easter Monday.

Sometimes, while Paul was still in England, we would go to spend Christmas with the McNeillys at Ms. Roe's Boarding House at Westbourne Square. Aunt May and her children (John, Esmee and Jean) lived in some rooms at the very top of the house. I don't remember much about it except that there were endless stairs and we had to put a shilling in the meter to get hot water for our weekly bath. The drawing room was quite pleasant but the dining room/ kitchen in the basement was rather dark and depressing.

My other memory of Ms. Roe's was that on an occasion, Paul and I were invited by a fellow student to a birthday party in Merton Park. This involved getting to Edgeware Road by bus and then taking the tube to Morden on the Edgeware-Morden Line, then a bus to our destination. After the party–and it was a good party with plenty to eat–we had to retrace our steps. I slept fitfully on the tube, confident that big brother was checking the stations. I was awakened and stepped off thinking that the station seemed unfamiliar. We went up a lift and exited to unfamiliar surroundings. It then dawned on us that we were at Edgeware–out in the country. We hastily turned back, only to be told that that had been the last train. The stationmaster was just shutting up. He did direct us that if we walked a mile or two in a certain direction we might catch a tram. We were lucky, and did . . . and luckily we had the few pennies needed, but when we got back to Edgeware Road, the last bus had gone so we had to walk to Westbourne Square. As we got there at around 1:00 a.m., Ms. Roe had long since locked up and everybody had gone to bed. The intrepid Paul climbed over the railings and was endeavouring to push up the drawing room window when we heard, "'Allo! 'Allo! 'Allo!" and turned to see a bobby. Paul hastily explained the circumstances but we had to ring and knock and get Ms. Roe up to identify us and have us released from custody.

My stay at Emmanuel School was uneventful. I was put into 3rd Modern; the other choices being Literature or Science. The school was a massive stone structure standing on modest grounds between two sets of railroad tracks at Clapham Junction. For the first week I heard the whistle of the trains and the clack of the wheels but after that I was not conscious of them.

Our headmaster was a rather severe gentleman called Dr. Broome. I have an image of him flying along the corridors with gown streaming horizontally behind him. My only other memory of him is when–as school ended for the day and I was getting books out of my desk–a chair leg crashed on the wall beside my head. I was so furious that I picked it up and threw it blindly, barely missing the hand that gripped the classroom door. You can guess who came in. "Who threw that!?"

"I did, sir," I said meekly.

"Stand up when you're spoken to, b'y!" He never said boy; always b'y!

I shot to my feet.

"Take three detentions and a caning!" and away he sailed.

Detention meant that I had to walk a half-mile to Wimbledon Station, take a train to Clapham Junction, walk another half-mile to the school and waste my whole Saturday morning thus. I submitted on the first Saturday, but on the second, I plucked up my courage and knocked on the big oak door to the headmaster's study and begged off. When he heard the circumstances, he let me off. I never did have the caning.

It was at Emmanuel that I was introduced to rugger. I took to it like a duck to water. I got onto a form team and played a few games that merely whetted my appetite for the game. I also took up cross-country running but there was little enthusiasm for either.

In the spring of 1935 came the news that Paul (who was graduating from Emmanuel) and I would be going home for the summer . . . and I could invite Tom. What excitement! We all had return-tickets as Paul was to return to study engineering, I was going back to school, and Tom was returning to his family. As it turned out, Paul discovered that Daddy's finances were in a parlous state, as he had mortgaged everything he had (including Morne Fendue) to Hankeys for the purchase of the Carriacou properties, which were losing money. Daddy was in danger of losing everything. Being the kind, generous person Paul was, he decided that he would not add to the indebtedness by returning to pursue his engineering studies. He went to Carriacou and took over management of the estates instead.

Mr. Kilby had escorted us by train to Portsmouth and saw us embark on the Royal Netherlands Steamship Co. vessel, *SS Crijnssen* for Trinidad. The attraction of the *Crijnssen* was that they offered student passages for £15, return. No matter that she did not call at Grenada. Deck passages could be had for a few pounds on one of the Lady Boats from Trinidad to Grenada.

On the first morning out we forgot to put back our watches, so we came out at eight o'clock for breakfast to find a deserted ship. It took us a while to learn that it was but six o'clock, "ship's time." We were in the Bay of Biscay and I still remember the long rollers that the ship had to climb, then coast down the other side of. By the time the saloon was ready for breakfast we were all a little queasy. When fried eggs arrived there was a steady exodus until only Tom remained. We soon found out from Mr. Gittens Knight, who was in first class, that the food was the same in both classes. Only the accommodations were different. We had shuffleboard and bridge and were quite content with our lot.

We found that we were all three in the same cabin, which suited us fine. We were all crazy about bridge so if we found that we were all awake at 2:00 a.m. or 4:00 a.m. we would sit up and play three-handed. What fun we had!

The *Crijnssen* stopped in St. Vincent to unload cargo and we were thrilled when Mr. Knight asked if we wished to accompany him ashore. He had some friends there and proposed visiting them. Meanwhile we were intrigued to watch the boys who would dive from their row boats to recover any coins that the other passengers (who had some to spare) threw into the water near them. Mr. Knight hired one of these boats–for a shilling–and we were rowed ashore in style. We went to the police station (call boxes were unheard of) and called his friend, Dr. Charles. He put on an exaggerated Oxford accent, told Dr. Charles that he was Prince So and So from Ghana and that he had met his friend Gittens Knight in London and promised to call when passing through. Dr. Charles said he would send his car for him . . . and did. When we got to the Charles' home, we were greeted by Dr. and Mrs. Charles in full evening dress. We had a good laugh and a good meal, and were very grateful for the interlude.

We sailed that night and by morning were into The Gulf of Paria. Tony Bishop's father, Dr. Bishop (who had been a medical practitioner in Gouyave and had gotten friendly with my parents) met us and we overnighted with them. The next day we were shipped on to Grenada. Daddy met us with the old Pontiac–with a cloth roof that could be put down–and we were driven to Morne Fendue. Apart from Mother and Daddy, I remember Betty and Gwen being there, also Winifred Glean, for some of the time. Others in the parish were Gordon Gentle (who was managing Madeys for Aunt Nellie), Eric Copland, Alister Glean, Willie McNeilly and Noel Button (a young Englishman who was visiting Canon Gough, the resident Anglican priest).

The holiday is a bit of a blur of picnics and parties and tennis and horse-riding and swimming, and an atmosphere so alien to my austere life in England that I couldn't contemplate returning with any pleasure. Indeed I was almost relieved when I developed a boil on my inner thigh–supposedly trying to start Willie's BSA motorcycle. He had told me that if I could start it, I could ride it. Of course I was the whippersnapper, three years younger than Paul and even more than the others, but I was always striving to keep up with them. As a result of the boil, Tom and I did not return to England until early October. Paul had decided to stay and endeavour to repair the family finances, noble fellow! Tom and I went back to Trinidad and again stayed with the Bishops. We embarked on the Royal Navy Ship, *The Venezuela* for the return journey and landed at Plymouth. I remember the beauty of the autumn trees on the train journey to London.

I stayed with Jocelyn and Teddy and returned to Emmanuel for the rest of the term but it had already been decided that I should go to a boarding school. So, one day Teddy took me by train to Bedford to be interviewed by Mr. W.H. Liddle, Headmaster of Bedford Modern School. His study was rather severe with a large oaken desk and large leather chairs. As I had been coached to be on my best behaviour, I tried sitting back but found I was almost horizontal, so decided it was more appropriate to the situation to perch. Mr. Liddle was quite friendly and pleasant, so when he asked Teddy Forshaw, "Does he have a sense of humour?" I smiled. Mr. Liddle had turned to look at me, and without waiting for an answer said, "We'll take him!" I didn't know in the least, what I was getting into, so didn't know whether to be glad or sorry.

I'm not sure just at what stage I transferred from boarding at Birnam to Mrs. Mann, who lived just around the corner at 27 Dorset Road. I think this was shortly after I returned from the West Indies. Mrs. Mann was a dear lady. Her husband, a bank manager, had died early leaving her with three teenage children. The eldest, John, had had to leave Taunton School to take up employment with National Provincial Bank. I think Barbara was similarly employed and the youngest was at school. I paid her 30 shillings per week for board and lodging. She had two or three other (elderly) boarders. There was a lady who spent the first few days asking me, "Edward! What food do you eat in India? . . . What clothes do you wear in India? . . . What sort of houses do you live in, in India?" Protestations that I was from the West Indies; In the Gulf of Mexico! Between North and South America! had no effect, but she eventually gave up. Mr. Hunt was a dear gentleman, recently retired from a wool house in the city. This led me to believe that he was just past the age of sixty. On that first Christmas he bought two cherry-wood pipes and two tins of Bell's Three Nuns tobacco for John and I, and insisted that we light up with him in the evenings. There was much coughing and spluttering and neither of us really took to it. There was also a gentleman who restored valuable paintings and thought rather well of himself as a consequence. I had a brush with him when he asserted that pineapples grew under the ground–like potatoes. I foolishly tried to put him right and earned his wrath. I steered clear of him after that and don't remember his name. But everybody else was very nice to me. I had a room to myself but we all shared the bathroom. The drawing room was comfortable and there was a garden with some fruit trees. Mrs. Mann fed us well and it was a pleasant place to stay.

Mother was convinced that Daddy had no sense of the value of money but was determined that Paul and I should. She arranged, through Daddy, that Hankeys should send me a cheque for £15 at the end of each month. An account was opened at National Provincial Bank and I was given a cheque book. I was but fifteen years old, and from this I had to send Jocelyn £2 10s per month (Hankeys would not have agreed to sending her money). From the remaining £150 per annum, I had to pay school fees of £6 10s and boarding fees of £32 per term and pay for my clothes, travelling, holiday boarding and pocket money (one shilling per week during school time, and five shillings per week during holidays). How I managed I don't know as there were no postal orders from home and no extras from Hankeys. But manage I did, and if today I am frugal I think the readers will understand why.

My memory of my arrival at School House (1 Warwick Avenue) is somewhat hazy. I guess Teddy Forshaw must have escorted me, but I do not remember him on that journey. Perhaps I was too apprehensive. I was going to a strange environment where I knew nobody. I do remember going to St. Pancras; taking a taxi (a rare occasion indeed) and being introduced–or handed over–to Ms. Bourne, Matron at School House. Why I arrived on a Wednesday in the middle of January, I cannot say. Perhaps there was a muddle about getting money from Hankeys to pay the school and boarding fees. But that I arrived on a Wednesday, there can be no doubt. I was put in the charge of two boarders who explained that there was a half-day school on Wednesdays; they were going into town . . . would I like to go with them? For sure. School House was about a mile from the school itself and I was glad of their companionship so off we went.

This was my introduction to the very strict rules of conduct for "day boys" and boarders alike. I think I remember them all but at this outset the relevant ones were, "during term, no boy will appear in public without his school uniform" (grey bags, sport jacket, black shoes, starched collar and school tie). To crown it all was the school cap that perched on the back of the wearer's head with the small peak in the centre. I was instructed that boys were not permitted to walk with their hands in their pockets, or eat sweets in the street, or walk on the pavement three abreast. Later I found out that boys were not permitted to talk to girls in the street, but at this stage I was far from committing this crime. I had memorized the last rule, that "conduct detrimental to the good name of the school is punishable as such," so decided to step warily.

Being properly attired we proceeded into town–in a 2:1 formation–and I breathed a sigh of relief when we turned into Woolworths, which was right opposite the school's side entrance, without apparently infringing any rules. I did not have any spare cash to buy anything but followed my companions who suddenly froze. I followed their gaze and saw a figure in a cap, gown streaming behind him, bearing down on us. Before I could say a word, I found myself handed over to a master in a school classroom. He was supervising detention. My companions were quickly seated and put to some task. The master looked me over quizzically and asked if I was a new boy. I confessed that I was. "Did you know that boys are not permitted to enter Woolworths and/or Marks & Spencers without their housemaster's written permission?" "I did not," being careful to say, ". . . sir!" I was made to understand that I was excused because of my ignorance. Fortunately, I had noted the route and was able to find my way back to the sanctuary of School House. This was my introduction to Bedford Modern School. It left me rather apprehensive.

I soon found out that School House was one of the two homes for some 72 boarders. The other was Stanford House. Together we formed one of the six houses; North, South, East, West, County and Boarders. All of the other 630 pupils were "day boys." Boys were allocated houses according to where their parents lived. School House occupied two-thirds of a large residence. The other third was occupied by the headmaster, Mr. Liddle and his wife and three children. Our section was controlled by the housemaster, Mr. Thornton, the matron, Ms. Borne, and the Head of House. There were 32 pupils spread between The Library (Head of House and two deputies), Senior Study (6), The Hall (16), and Junior Study (7).

Ms. Bourne was a rather formidable critter who I best remember for her admonition that you went to her for her to tell you what was wrong with you. Not the other way 'round. Being a nondescript character, I was assigned to The Hall and slept in the senior dormitory which was ruled by Head of House. My dormitory was a large open room with sixteen beds and three large windows which were open night and day, summer and winter (unless rain or snow was blowing in). In due course I found that this was not a house rule, but schoolboy heroics. Considering that the bed covering consisted of three thin blankets and a sheet, these were pretty spartan conditions. However, I soon found that a four-mile cross-country run or a game of rugger warmed the blood and kept out the cold.

The boys were friendly and there was no bullying, but I was introduced to the "fagging" or "junior" system. Six of the youngest boys were designated as juniors. If the Head of House or either of the two deputies wanted their shoes blacked–brown shoes were forbidden–or something fetched, then he would open the library door, shout, "Junior!" and wait. The last of the six to arrive was given the task. These were never very onerous and the commission was just accepted as a way of life and the task was always done cheerfully. Strangely there was no animosity.

After a spartan breakfast (slices of fried tomato or green peas on lightly toasted bread with an abundance of bread, butter and marmalade, and hot cocoa) the boys walked to school. The hours were from 9:00 a.m. to noon, and 1:30 p.m. to 4:00 p.m. in the summer, but in the winter the hours were 9:00 a.m. to noon and 3:00 p.m. to 5:30 p.m. This was to allow games to be played whilst there was still daylight. Boarders were not allowed to ride bikes to school, but many Day Boys did.

There was just time to walk back to the house for lunch and back to the school for afternoon classes. The Headmaster and family came in for lunch with the boys each day. He and the rest of his family presided over the top table, Mrs. Liddle ruled over the next and Mr. Thornton over the other. It was not long before (as Head of Study) I had to sit at the end of the top table and spoon out the meat or dessert, with one of my colleagues kicking me under the table to protest that I was giving out too much . . . there wouldn't be enough left for us. But in those early days I sat at Mrs. Liddle's table. She expressed herself as being very impressed by my good manners–Morne Fendue training–and I became something of a teacher's pet. On an occasion when I was the only one to go down with mumps, she put me in her spare bedroom and was most solicitous.

The whole house assembled for meals in The Hall. Breakfast at 8:00 a.m., lunch at 12:20 p.m., tea at 5:00 p.m. and supper at 7:00 p.m. At this last meal, Mr. Thornton presided and said the grace, which sounded like *Peasum Christum Dominum Nostrum.* No one knew what it meant and no one enquired. We had hot chocolate and biscuits and then the boys of the Junior Study retired to their domain. Prep went on to 9:00 p.m. and then the boys of The Hall retired to bed. The Head of House and his two deputies–who occupied the library–were permitted to stay up 'till 10:00 p.m.

After my first term, our matron was replaced by Miss Peggy Bitton, who was slight in body, but a great matron. She tended to the needs of the boys with sympathy and dedication, and helped me out of many a scrape.

When I became Head of Study (there were five others) I persuaded the others to each put up 6p on the first Saturday, and with that we bought a frying pan and utensils, and the next Saturday we had our first feast. We could get bread, butter, milk and sugar from the kitchen staff, so we bought a dozen eggs, a couple pounds of sausages, some tomatoes and some lemons, with which I made lemonade, and continued to have a feast every Saturday for the rest of the year. The boys were amazed that lemons could so easily be converted into lemonade.

The catering at School House was the responsibility of Mrs. Liddle, the headmaster's wife. The food was barely sufficient for 18-year-old schoolboys playing a lot of sport, but there was a plentiful supply of bread, butter, milk and marmalade. And since we frequently had green peas or sliced tomato on toast (wet bread really) we made up with bread and marmalade. There was a system of petty cash, by which the Head of House went around on Friday evenings to ask if anyone wanted 6p for a haircut or a comb, or whatever excuse could be thought of, to get an additional amount to the one shilling pocket money given to each boy, regardless of age. One September, we found out that the marmalade was a homemade brew. It was rumoured that Mrs. Liddle had gotten a job-lot of grapefruit and had the kitchen staff making marmalade all summer. It was not to my liking. When I was Head of Study and term recommenced, the Head of House came to me first and I said I needed nothing. Then I said, "Oh yes, put me down for one shilling, for a pot of marmalade." As he went to the other 30 boys in the house, each one took the cue from me and put down a shilling for a pot of marmalade. After supper that evening, Mr. Thornton was furious and said that no one would get pocket money the following day, unless they came to apologise. So after supper, instead of resuming prep/homework, the whole house congregated outside his door, and being the senior, I went in first. I pretended to not understand quite why he wanted to see me, and said that I was sure that it was excellent marmalade, but I just did not like it. He responded, "No Kent, it's not good enough; it's a conspiracy!" I protested, "No sir, it's not a conspiracy! Crosher came to me first, as head of study, and I asked for a shilling for marmalade. I suppose the other boys saw this and did the same!" He shook his head and dismissed me. The other boys went in, one by one, and apologized. The last junior came out and reported that Mr. Thornton had said in his presence, "I am utterly defeated, the army is too strong!" We did get our pocket money next day, but not the extra for marmalade. No more was said about marmalade!

School House was a happy house. There was a great *esprit de corps*, no bullying, though there was a system of "juniors," or *fags* as they were called in Dickens' time. Shortly after I became Head of House (September 1937) as I passed the changing room I heard a sniffling. I found a boy of about 11 years, born of English parents and raised in India, who had often brought him to England on holiday. On that day they had sailed for India and he felt utterly alone. I took him to the tuck shop and bought him an ice cream and he became my willing "slave" thereafter.

When I became Head of House I bought a bell and battery and rigged it up so that I could sit by my fire and just press a button, there would be a mad stampede and a knocking on the door and I would ask for whatever I wanted brought!

One evening when we assembled in The Hall for supper, there was a big splash of ink on the white ceiling. After prayers Mr. Thornton, the housemaster, required that whoever was responsible was to report to him in his room. No one did, so the next evening he was a bit more demanding and threatening, but still no one reported. At this stage he handed over the investigation to me, as Head of House, and I announced that no one would be allowed out for the fifty-minute break between tea and lock-up until someone had owned up. No one did, and this went on for several days, until the headmaster sent for me and said, "Oh Kent! It is time to forget about this; just give the house a punishment and then forget it." So that evening after tea, we lined the boys up in a circle in the quad and ran them around for 20 minutes. I had told the headmaster that this would be taken as a joke by School House, and so it was. That evening after prayers and after the housemaster had left, I said that I was puzzled that any member of School House would let all the boys suffer for the better part of a week without owning up. There would be no punishment, but I hoped that somebody would explain to me what had happened. Shortly after, there was a knock on the library door and the boy who I had befriended (from the change room) came to tell me that some boys had been ragging and they had knocked an ink well with a broken lip off a bench. It had fallen and the ink had splashed up onto the ceiling. I scoffed at this, and sent him to bring the ink well. It did indeed have a broken lip so I asked, "How much ink did it have in it? Half an inch?" And seated before the fire, I said, "Let us drop it and see what happens! Is this the height of the bench?" He agreed, so I dropped it and ink flew up all over me, the mantelpiece and the ceiling! I, of course, rushed to the matron for help and she put my pants and shirt to soak. The other boys rallied 'round and we found in the cellar a roll of matching wallpaper. They got flour from the kitchen to make a paste and re-papered the mantelpiece. We collected all the blanco from OTC members and whitewashed the ceiling. Matron advised me to tell Mrs. Liddle what had happened. She assured me that if I did, Mrs. Liddle would not be angry, but if I did not and she found out, she would be very angry indeed. I met Mrs. Liddle on the landing shortly after, and with my heart in my boots, confessed. She gave a little giggle and said, "Oh Kent, I am so glad you told me, I am just going to Cambridge to see my parents. Toodleoo!"

One September, we found that every morning we were given three crab-apples. We saved these all during the week, and on Saturday, we would crush them and strain the juice through a carefully washed handkerchief, and save it till we had a cider-bottle full of our juice. This was buried in the garden to mature.

At the beginning of the next term one Saturday evening, we decided to check on the cider and we were just preparing to do so when Mr. Thornton knocked on the door and said, "Kent, the headmaster wants to see you in his study." When I went in, he was sitting at his desk writing, and said, "Kent, have a seat." So with trepidation, I sat perched on one of the big leather armchairs, and waited. After a while, he took off his glasses and glared at me and said, "Kent, I understand you are leaving school at the end of this term. Why are you leaving?"

"Why sir, I have done my school certificate, and the price of cocoa is not good, and I think it is time I should go to help my parents."

"Nonsense," he said. "Can you pay the school fees?"

The school fees were £6 10s per term, whilst the boarding fees were £32 per term. I said, "I think I might, sir."

"Well, come back for another year. Don't bother about the boarding fees, just pay the school fees."

And so I did. But when I returned from the headmaster`s study, I found panic stations–the cider bottle had been opened in my absence, and the cider had jetted out, halfway across the ceiling, so there was a great clearing up in process which took several hours.

In 1936 when I joined Bedford Modern School it was not in the top echelon of public schools, but our headmaster, Mr. Liddle was determined to get it there. This was to be achieved by excellence in sport, so we were required to row at Henley, participate in the public school sports at White City, play water polo against Cambridge Colleges, and rugger against the best schools and clubs from London. So there was far more emphasis placed on sporting activities than on academics. When we were approaching school certificates, the headmaster came to the gym one day and required each boy to do a vault, and he just stood there saying, "pass, pass, fail, pass, fail . . . " as he maintained that if your brain and your muscles were well coordinated, and you had done nine years of schooling, you did not do any extra studying to pass exams! We soon proved him wrong, because a bunch of us failed to pass the required five subjects, (I passed four) and we were put into a 5th Removed, and sat the exam again the following November, when 31 of the boys in the form passed well. I then went into form 6th Literature, where we studied economics and had an excellent master. For the first time in my school career, I really took a liking to academic studies, and was much looking forward to going to university. At this time I wrote Mother asking if I might take piano lessons, but to my dismay she replied that I should take extra lessons in Latin, since I was destined to study law. It was with a heavy heart that I left school in July 1939.

I wrote to Thomson Hankey & Co., asking for extra money to pay my passage home. They replied that they had no such instruction from Mr. George Kent, but if I would make a booking, they would pay for the ticket and send me £5 extra. I booked on the Royal

Netherlands Steamship Co. *SS Crijnssen*, which took me to Trinidad. We were barely south of the Azores when the ship's telegraph picked up word of the declaration of war with Germany. As the Netherlands was neutral at the time, the captain put up and floodlit a large Dutch flag–we found out later that there were many German submarines in the area.

On arrival in Trinidad, I had to pay a boat to take me ashore, which left me penniless, and there was no one to meet me. So I started walking up Frederick Street when I heard a shout and it was Gladys Glean who was coming to meet me, as Gwen was working. Gladys took me to the Copland's home, where I met Isabel. I only had warm clothes, and it was hot, and I felt I would die. They must have lent me some money, because I got passage on a Lady Boat to Grenada. The Lady Boats traded between Canada and Trinidad and the islands in between. It was with relief that I landed in Grenada, and cannot remember who met me, but I remember getting the news that the whole family was in Carriacou.

Where I stayed in St. George's I cannot remember, but shortly after, I went up to Carriacou on a sailing boat to meet my family at Craigston. There were Mother and Daddy, Betty and Paul. I returned to Morne Fendue with the family and enjoyed some weeks of holiday, and then gave thought to returning to England where many of my friends had gone into the armed services. I had left England with a return ticket, the intention being to start my law studies, but I soon found that it was necessary to have a medical examination, as one could only return if one could go into the armed services. The senior medical officer, an Englishman called Dr. Cochran, said after my examination, "Boy, you're the fittest young man I have examined, but you only have one eye, and I cannot pass you." Several of my friends applied to the Canadian Armed Forces and again, I went for a medical, with the same result.

My parents, George and Louisa Beatrice Kent

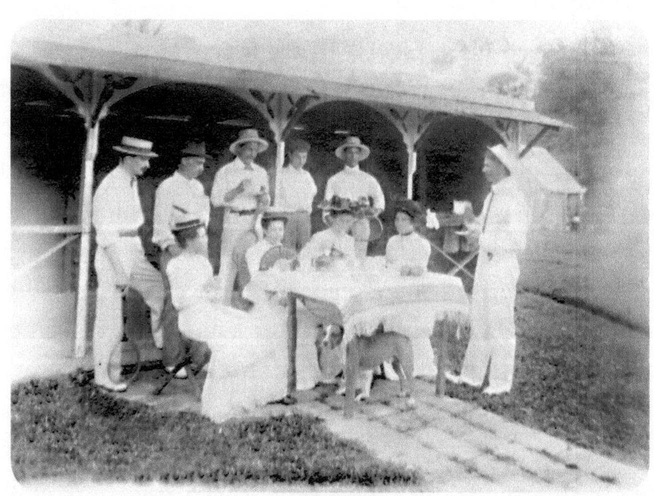

St. Patrick's Tennis Club. My father George (far right) and his brother Fred (centre) back row.

St. Patrick's 'ball boy' in full tennis kit

At Kew Gardens

Embarking on SS Crijnssen at Portsmouth (to Grenada) with Paul and Tom Kilby

"Under the trees" at Morne Fendue. Paul and I with our parents and sisters Betty and Gwen.

Carriacou

('till this thing blows over)

I started looking for a job in Grenada, and was told by Superintendent of Public Works, Mr. Clarrie Renwick, that he would give me a job as a road overseer, but I would have to supply my own transport. I negotiated with McIntyre Bros. for the purchase of a motorcycle on terms, and reported my readiness to Mr. Renwick. He demurred for some weeks, and then explained that some members of staff of Public Works Dept. were complaining that they were denied a chance of promotion by the recruitment of untrained persons.

Fortunately, the motorcycle had been little used, and McIntyre Bros. agreed to take it back without penalty.

During this period, there was a series of activities at the plantation houses to raise money to either buy a Spitfire, or for the Red Cross. My cousin Gordon Gentle had returned from school in England two or three years before and had been "adopted" by his Aunt Nellie Gill to manage Madeys Estate. He had a BSA sports car, and he and I were the "Men About Town." I think it was after some such party that the next morning my father said to me, without leaving room for argument, "Edward, I think you'd better go to Carriacou for a few weeks until this thing blows over."

I packed the few possessions I had and took the *MV Enterprise* (the mail service at the time, owned by Conway Steele, with Sandow Glean as engineer). She left St. George's at 8:00 a.m. every Monday, and those boarding from Sauteurs were "stood-by" at ten o'clock in a fishing boat on the beach at Sauteurs, waiting for the first sign of her coming around Tanga Langa Point. As soon as she was seen, the fishermen pushed the boat out into the waves–the sea was always rough–and skilfully got the boat beyond the rollers without being swamped. They rowed out to meet Enterprise, which hove-to, and passengers scrambled onboard while luggage was thrown up on deck. Depending upon the vagaries of wind and tide and engine, with luck, Enterprise got to Carriacou around 4:00 p.m. The schooner did not come alongside but passengers were ferried ashore by bumboats.

Brother Paul met me with the old Pontiac car which Daddy had shipped to Carriacou when it was past its best days. John Copeland was the engineer at Craigston, and John and Paul were in residence at Craigston and I joined them. The house was the same wooden house that I had first known in 1927 but cotton was the main crop grown back in those days–though Craigston and Dumfries Estates had, or were converting to limes. As cotton required full sunlight there were few trees (except on the higher lands) but there was cotton everywhere, even between the rows of limes.

The house was like a big bungalow elevated on 7' stone walls that enclosed an enormous cellar. There were but three bedrooms and separate dining and living rooms, with a wide verandah running 'round three sides and a detached kitchen and "Servants Quarters." The furniture was adequate but sparse. Back in the days when the Archer family owned the house there was a stable with three horses and a groom named Whittaker, who had been brought from Barbados by Tom and Thelma Archer, and left when Tom Archer lost the estates. In the front was an enormous cistern that stored the rain water collected off the roof. Carriacou has no rivers so the population subsists on rain water, and the animals for the most part, on well water. Much later we learned that the cistern had been built between 1782 and 1786.

There were beautiful views down over the harbour to the south and another over the lower lands of the estate to Sparrow Bay, and right up to Union Island. The whole island was much more open in those days. It had been deforested to provide firewood for the boilers of the sugar factories in the days of sugar cane, and indeed the slaves had been required to clear the upper slopes–not suitable for sugar–to grow crops for their own subsistence. A census of 1792 shows that there were only 700 acres of uncultivated land on Carriacou back then. The slopes were planted in corn, peas, and cotton which required much hoeing in their cultivation. The soil was generally bare during the dry season so that three or four inches of rain would result in tremendous run off and erosion. This was evident throughout the island but nowhere more so than in the Belmont area where peanuts were grown extensively. The peanut requires the forking up of the earth for harvest. The earth remained bare and subject to wind erosion during the last three months of the dry season, then, when the rains came there were neither crops nor weeds to bind the soil and it washed into the sea in large quantities.

The first job that I was assigned to by my brother Paul, who was manager, was to go out with a pruning gang in Beausejour, led by a

Vincentian named Mr. Quammie. Work started at 7:00 a.m. sharp! Paul was punctilious in his punctuality. Whistles were blown at noon, when we walked home for a hurried lunch, and walked back to wherever we were working, to resume promptly at 1:00 p.m. Without any shade from the lime trees, and with the brief transition from the climate of Britain, I found the heat almost unbearable, but remembered the admonition of Mr. Liddle at Bedford Modern School, who, just before caning boys would say, "Grin and bear it, grin and bear it. Be a man."

It was important to gain respect, thus authority, and to show that I could do–or stand–what the workers could. The pruning gang consisted of about twenty young men who sawed off the dead limbs and cut off the superfluous suckers with secateurs. Some used long forked sticks to heap up the limbs for burning, or to push them into the roaring fires. It was already very hot and to get near to these fires was additional torture. The only concession to human weakness was that a woman designated as "water carrier" was assigned to draw water from one of the cisterns and carry it on her head in a kerosene tin to the various gangs where thirsty workers would pluck a large leaf which she would fill with water from a dipper. The dipper was usually a small bowley attached to a short stick that enabled her to dip from the kerosene tin without removing it from her head. When her tin was empty, she walked back to the factory to refill it and then continued on her rounds. Ice was unheard of.

The lime trees were attacked by lime borer which laid their eggs in the branches. When the larvae hatched, they worked their way along the core of the branch until they emerged many feet along. To a casual observer the branch looked healthy but in any heavy wind or when laden with fruit, it would break. In the dry season all these limbs were cut off and burnt in an effort to destroy as many of these pests as possible. In the 30s and 40s there were at least a dozen tanks on wheels equipped with long lances for spraying lime trees for borer and blight. An elderly man told me that his first job was collecting conger eels up in Prospect–at 4p per kerosene tin–for Mr. Archer to release in the lime fields to, "eat the blight." The tanks on wheels were loaded with Bordeaux Mixture (a compound of soap and copper sulphate and water) which was reputed to smother the mealy bug that infested the lime leaves and exuded a waxy substance on which the black fungus lived. This black fungus covered the lime leaves thus inhibiting photosynthesis. There was a large iron tank mounted on a steel frame which was filled with Bordeaux Mixture and taken out into the fields on the ox-drawn wagon to refill the spray tanks.

Shortly after I joined, John Copeland left, and James Cyrus from Bogles was appointed Chief Mechanic at the princely sum of 25 shillings per week. I received the princely sum of XCD (Eastern Caribbean Dollars) $23 per month and gave my mother $21 toward by board. This left me with $2 a month, but I really had nothing on which to spend any money. As my father had mortgaged everything he owned, including Morne Fendue, and as the Carriacou estates were losing money (despite Paul only drawing XCD $45 per month as manager, and workers being paid one shilling per day for men, and 10p per day for women) and falling further and further into Hankey's debt. As they had foreclosed on the previous owner, it seemed likely that they would soon foreclose on my father, so it became imperative that every lime be collected, every drop of juice extracted and every ounce of oil recovered and sold.

During this period, Mother, who loved Carriacou, would frequently come up on the *Enterprise* for a month or six weeks before returning to look after Morne Fendue and Daddy. Mother had decided wisely that there was no need for two sons to be on Carriacou and so it was arranged that Paul should go to Trinidad to seek employment. On the 3rd of March 1941, Paul left Carriacou for Gola where he worked for the Shell Oil Company for some years, until he returned to Grenada. I found myself at the tender age of 20, in charge of Craigston Estates and all the machinery therein. The machinery in the factory consisted of an old Tangie engine that drank kerosene, a small Petter 6hp diesel engine that by contrast was the epitome of efficiency and which drove the two cane mills used for crushing limes, the boiler, an injector and the whisky still, which was used to distill lime oil.

Craigston Lime Factory

Craigston Factory Storeroom

The Lime Industry
and Craigston Estate

The Lime industry was started on Carriacou early in the 20th century by Mr. Tom Archer, whose wife Thelma inherited the estates of Craigston, Prospect, Limlair and Grand Bay from her uncle, James (John Mill). Years ago I met an elderly man who told me that his father had brought the plants from Trinidad on his schooner.

Prior to the introduction of limes the main crop on the estates (and on Carriacou in general) had been cotton, but the Marie Galante variety grown on Carriacou is a short staple lint of inferior quality and with the development of large tracts of mechanically tilled and planted cotton on North America and Egypt, the price obtained for Carriacou cotton became less and less attractive, and it became uneconomic for the estates to pay labour to cultivate and harvest cotton. The remaining estates (The Dumfries Group–Dumfries, Lauriston, Breteche & Sabazan) and the Craigston Group let gardens to the workers on the métairie system, by which no rent was paid in cash but the estate claimed one-third of the cotton crop in lieu of rent. Every year, after the cotton crop was harvested, all animals were let loose (the Let-Go Season) to roam freely through the fields and strip the cotton shrubs of every leaf. The goats even ate some of the bark. To a degree, the droppings from these animals helped to fertilise the fields in preparation for the next crop. Toward the end of the dry season the remains of the cotton bushes were chopped, heaped and burnt to make way for the corn and peas that would be planted between the stools. The pigeon pea, being a nitrogenous plant, also helped to supply nitrogen for the ensuing crop.

In the 1930s there were cotton ginneries at Dumfries, Mt. Pleasant, Craigston and two in Hillsborough. Some 1,300 bales, each of 300 lbs. of lint were exported to England. The seed was exported to the factories in Barbados and/or Antigua for manufacture of cooking oil. In the 1930s a co-op was formed and ginning was confined to the ginnery in Hillsborough on the present-day site of the Carriacou Museum. Financing to pay a cash advance for the raw cotton was always a problem. The small farmers were often left with their harvested cotton stashed in their homes. Rats ate the seed in the lint and made nests, thereby staining the cotton and rendering it worthless. Farmers became discouraged and eventually the industry died.

Meanwhile, Mr. Archer had planted lime trees at Craigston and a lesser area at Grand Bay. Dumfries followed suit and much of the lower lands around the factory were planted in limes. A smaller area was planted at Lauriston. When production began, the limes were crushed with cane mills and the raw juice exported to England. Mr. Archer imported six coopers (with their families) and built a large coopering shed at the back (west) of the factory to make the oak barrels in which the juice was shipped. He also had built what at that time were the largest schooners ever built on Carriacou. One was appropriately named *The Thelma Archer*, and the other, *The Muriel Archer*. They carried supplies from Grenada and shipped lime juice to St. George's, but their main employment was in hauling molasses from Barbados to supply the rum still that Mr. Archer imported and had erected at Craigston in 1921. This was in fact a whiskey still made by Blair, Campbell & McLean of Glasgow, and was reputed to produce the finest rum in the colony. Mr. Archer also planted cane at Limlair for the production of molasses and although Limlair produced heavy yields, it was never enough to keep the distillery supplied. The cane was conveyed from Limlair to Craigston by oxcart and there, it was crushed and converted into rum.

I am uncertain just when Craigston discontinued the manufacture of rum. It is alleged that the Executive Council in Grenada passed legislation requiring all rum to be sold from the Government Bond in St. George's. The added cost, and the imposition of an import duty on molasses, made Craigston rum more expensive than rum produced in Grenada from locally grown cane. A Carriacou shopkeeper would have to sail to Grenada, make his purchase and then ship the casks back to Carriacou. This put Craigston at a considerable disadvantage and, coupled with the ban on importation of molasses, led to the discontinuance of the production of rum at Craigston. For sure, by 1927 when the estates were purchased from Thomson Hankey & Co. by Mr. George Kent of St. Patrick's, Grenada, rum was no longer produced.

Records on hand (*gratis de* Tony Archer of British Columbia) indicate that the shipping of lime juice to the English market through Thomson Hankey and Co. was not a profitable undertaking. These records reveal that in 1920 Mr. Archer shipped 653 barrels of lime juice to England through Hankeys. These yielded a gross return of £2,193 2s 1p. Hankeys immediately claimed a 2.5% commission and deducted £54 16s 7p. After they had made further deductions for brokerage, freight, dock dues and port rates, insurance, fire insurance, interest on freight and dock dues, guarantee and commission (charged twice!) Mr. Archer's account was credited on 3rd February, 1920 with £6 10s 4p.

The shipment of lime juice had also been discontinued and the whiskey still was used exclusively for the production of lime oil. Since it had only been installed in 1921, its use for the manufacture of rum must have been brief. I am also uncertain just when Hankeys foreclosed on the Archers, but it was probably c. 1925/26.

The overseer, Mr. S.J. Quashie, was left as manager, with Mr. Haydock of Dumfries as attorney. I have been told that on an occasion, Mr. Haydock visited Craigston unexpectedly and found a large number of people in the factory yard. On enquiry he was told that Mr. Archer was selling off estate lands and they had come to buy. It was alleged that Mr. Archer got Mr. Quashie to see if he could get sufficient bookings for lands to be able to pay off the debt to Hankeys, or substantially reduce it so that he could regain possession. I think it was partly because of this that Mr. Quashie was dismissed and replaced by George La Barrie.

Mr. Barclay, manager of Hankeys in Grenada, recruited George La Barrie and got Mr. Haydock to offer him the job at Craigston. Mr. La Barrie has told me that he lived at Limlair, as after the Archers returned to Barbados, Craigston House was shut up for a time. It was reputed to be haunted. He explained also that the Catholic priest, Father Blenco had lived at Craigston House for a short while and did his best to dissuade him from moving there, because of it being haunted. According to George La Barrie, it was Father Blenco who built the chapel. Reputedly, Mrs. Archer–a devout Catholic–gave him permission. The people from the village of Bogles were almost exclusively Methodist, and he hoped to woo some of them to the Catholic faith. He actually held services there but before it was consecrated, Mr. Archer returned from a trip to England and forbade the holding of any more services there. When first I knew that building, there were small stone crosses at the gable ends and an oven had been built on. The roof was of slate. There was also a huge wooden cross with an effigy of Christ erected on the hill to the west of the Great House. Mrs. Archer, who was the legal owner of the estates, gave 2 acres of land on the southern boundary to the Catholic Church. A Presbytery was built there and that was where Father Thompson (followed by Father Devas) lived in 1940, when I came to live on Carriacou.

There are three buildings of similar size, shape and architecture as "The Chapel" on Carriacou; one at Belvedere, one at Dumfries, and the one at Craigston. Those at Belvedere and Dumfries are probably 200 years old or more. Is the Craigston Chapel only 80-odd years old? I think it more likely that Father Blenco converted the existing building into a chapel . . . if it wasn't one before. In the 40s, the old people referred to the building as The Pigeon House; possibly it was before Father Blenco converted it.

George La Barrie said that when there was distillation of lime oil taking place at Craigston–a 24-hour per day operation–he would frequently get wet riding home in the rain at night, so he got permission from Mr. Barclay of Hankeys to change and repair the house. It was he who transformed the house from a totally enclosed building (as is shown on the old plans and in the 1918 picture) to the house with wide-open verandahs on three sides, which was as I knew it in 1927, until 1955 when it was demolished by Hurricane Janet.

The house had no internal plumbing. There was a big brass hand pump on the wall closest to the cistern and a galvanized iron tank with a tap on a stand on the back verandah. Water for the house and kitchen was drawn off there. The concrete bath was down–almost at ground level. It had a big brass rose that gave a shower like being under a waterfall. Next door was a latrine that consisted of a bucket under a hole in the seat. Old newspaper (or other paper) substituted for toilet paper. A tin of ashes was provided and this was scattered liberally when the facility had been used. Every morning around dawn an old woman from the village took the bucket and dumped the contents in a pit dug at a distance from the house. She then covered the contents with earth. The ground floor of the house was one big room and two smaller ones. Here it was that the hogsheads of pigs' tails and salt beef were stored–to augment the slaves' rations in earlier times. The walls (20" thick, of stone with brick pillars to support the beams for the main floor) today support the house built in 1974. There are two arches that funnel cool air into the storerooms so that they always remain cool. In 1927, bags of provisions or fruit were stored there. Even the remains of 50 lb. blocks of ice (from Grenada) were stored in a barrel filled with sawdust and would last for a few days. As was traditional, the kitchen was a less substantial building, separated from the main house by about twenty feet. As fuel consisted of coals and firewood, it was located so that in the event of fire, it would burn without destroying the Great House. Generations of yard boys kept it supplied with fuel from the surrounding fields or forests.

The domestic water supply was drawn or pumped from the large cistern that lies immediately to the west of the house. Records from Craigston Castle (in Scotland) reveal that the excavation for the cistern was started by Mr. Arbuthnot, a relative of the Urquharts in 1782. In 1784 he was "sent home for giddiness," but was allowed to return to complete it in 1786.

The boiling house was added on in 1820 as evidenced by the keystone over the furnace door. It is inscribed, "I.U. 1820" which indicates the owner–Ian Urquhart–and the date of construction. Although the five copper *taitches* in which juice was boiled were indeed of copper, there were no limes growing in 1820 so we must presume that they were used for boiling down cane juice for the production of molasses and rum. There is no evidence that Craigston exported sugar, but the keystone on the furnace door indicates that sugar was made from 1820. We must presume that muscovado sugar was made and shipped to England in its raw state.

The *taitches* were lined off above a flue that led from the wood-fired furnace to the chimney, through the Boiling House to the wooden vats that sat on the lower floor, immediately to the north of the platform on which the still stands. The largest copper (250-gallon capacity) which received the cane or lime juice was situated over the fire. Next to it was one of 200-gallons and next to that was one of 150-gallons then one of 100-gallons, then the last of 50-gallons. This bank of *taitches* was not used in my time because neither Craigston, nor Dumfries were producing concentrated lime juice–except in 1945, just at the end of WWII when Dumfries was offered a contract to supply 250 pipes (105 gallons) of concentrated lime juice. As the Dumfries boiler had a leak, I wrote to my father seeking permission to allow Craigston to supply this order. Pending his decision, we had been saving all of the juice from the still, and as a result, we had a lake of lime juice that stretched from one end of the bank to the other. The *taitches* were all hidden by lime juice.

Word came from my father, refusing permission to supply concentrated lime juice because everything he tried at Craigston lost money. But in working out the cost of producing the concentrated lime juice, he included the cost of harvesting, processing, and even the cost of distilling. I wrote back a rather sharp letter pointing out that those costs had already been borne by producing the lime oil, so this was a product we were throwing away, and therefore we shouldn't include it in our costs. When I left out those costs, I calculated that we would make £250 on this contract. I signed my letter, "Yours Faithfully. . ." and my mother told me that this cut him to the quick. He was very hurt and said, "Okay, you do whatever you want." My father's apprehension to my request was an example of his lack of business sense and he was fearful of losing money again.

With my father's permission to proceed, the next Monday morning the furnace was lit for the first time in many years. Metan Stafford could not find any experienced furnace men, so engaged a young fellow to assist him. Metan spent the day stoking the boiler and coaching the new hand. At 4:00 p.m. the recruit announced that he had not come prepared to spend the night, so he left. Metan stoked the furnace for the whole night in spite of my urging him to go home. Next day the recruit fed the furnace under Metan's watchful eye, but again he quit at 4:00 p.m. Metan had been stoking the boiler for two days and the furnace for two nights, so I pleaded with him to, "close it down." He resisted all persuasion; said he just wanted to go home for an hour to change his clothes. I filled in with some help but he was soon back and continued to work day and night until Saturday. By this time the juice in the coppers was concentrated sufficiently for it to be casked and to permit the resumption of distillation. The casks were assembled from second-hand oak staves (and tops and bottoms imported from England or America) and flat iron strips, the ends of which were riveted together to make hoops that were driven down to squeeze the staves together to prevent leakage. Dried banana pseudostems were placed between the staves, like gaskets, and you could hear the rhythmic taps of an expert cooper as he went 'round and 'round the barrel, tapping the hoops lower and lower to tighten the joints, and occasionally giving a tap on the barrel top to keep the rhythm going.

The juice had to be concentrated to a certain specific gravity, by which time it was black. As the juice concentrated, it diminished in volume, so juice was ladled from one copper to the next and fresh juice added to the first. When the juice in the smallest copper had reached the required specific gravity, the furnace was allowed to cool down to allow the concentrated lime juice to cool a bit, then the dipper came into play. A substantial post was attached to the floor and beam alongside the smallest copper. A wooden arm was attached to it, and to this, a block and tackle, and cylindrical copper dipper with a valve on the bottom. When this was lowered into the smallest copper, the valve opened to permit it to be filled with concentrated lime juice. When it was lifted, the valve shut; the arm with the dipper was swung over the waiting cask into which was fitted a broad copper funnel. The valve was lifted slightly and the concentrated lime juice ran into the cask. The bungs were then hammered home with a wooden mallet; the casks had a number and "Craigston Estate" stenciled on, and were ready for shipment.

We fulfilled the contract and made a profit of some £250–a considerable sum in those days. Concentrated lime juice was used in England for the bleaching of wool and I guess that some synthetic product displaced the use of citric acid, as we never received another order.

It is difficult to remember that the whole area that housed the still, the boiler, the storage area where the vats for lime juice sat, the storeroom that sat over the six interconnected water tanks, and the two tanks to the west that supplied cooling water to the condenser and to the Wood House (where approximately 200 cords of firewood were accumulated and stored during the dry season) was enclosed by an enormous building, the roofs and walls of which were galvanized iron and scantling. The Distillery was like a house of cards with spindly uprights that were sometimes thirty feet tall. All braced and cross-braced with equally flimsy looking scantling. But it withstood the assault of Hurricane Hazel in 1944, although not Hurricane Janet in 1955. The roof and roofs of the main factory, boiler house and storeroom collected the water that filled the water tanks and enabled Craigston Factory to supply water not only to Bogles–which was perennial–but also to villages as far away as Windward and Grand Bay in a severe dry season.

George La Barrie claimed that when Mr. George Kent purchased the estates, he felt that his job was insecure as Mr. Kent had two sons who would, in time, displace him. He applied to Mr. George Gentle, Superintendent of Public Works, and was employed. This led to his being sent to Montserrat in charge of Public Works Dept. and his subsequent move to Antigua.

Shortly after Paul left for Trinidad, I noticed that the Mechanic, James Cyrus, was acting strangely, so I asked what was the matter.

He explained to me shyly that he had heard that the Americans, who were building the military bases in Trinidad, were paying good wages for pipe-fitters. James earned 25s per week with no overtime pay. Overtime was unheard of in those days. At Craigston management was required to have the skills not only of management, bookkeeping, accountancy, electricity, carpentry, masonry, pipefitting and whatever else, there was no one to call upon for assistance. But I couldn't raise James' pay so I had to swallow my dismay and let him go with a good recommendation and best wishes. I said, "Well James, I know you have a family, and I cannot afford to pay you any more, so I am sorry to see you go to Trinidad. But do you know anyone who knows anything about machinery?" I was the first to admit that coming from Public School in England, I knew little. He told me that there was a man who had worked in the oil fields of Maracaibo, Venezuela. I asked, "What is his name?"

"Metan Stafford," he replied.

I asked James where he was working and he told me he was digging drains. I said, "Please go and fetch him."

Metan and I thus started an association that lasted forty years. He turned out to be the most conscientious, dedicated, hard-working and capable employee that I ever had, and truly, I could not have processed the whole crop–without losing a pound of limes, a gallon of juice or an ounce of lime oil–without his unswerving help.

Metan had gone to Venezuela when some islanders were recruited to work in the oil refineries there. When their contract ended, they were given railway tickets to the port to catch a vessel to take them home. He and some other small islanders took the wrong way and went up into the hinterland where the Venezuelans were drilling for oil. He had somehow acquired a truck and the authorities supplied him with fuel, oil and tyres, and paid him to freight for them. He prospered for several years until he had two shops, then one day the *gendarmerie* rounded up 15 small-islanders who were in the country illegally, imprisoned them for nine months without access to their

Consular Agents, lawyers, or any form of trial. Then they were taken to a point off the south coast of Trinidad where they were made to undress, put their clothes on their heads and swim or wade to the Trinidad shore. In due course, Metan boarded one of the Carriacou sloops that plied between Carriacou, Grenada and Trinidad and came home. He valued the property he left behind at XCD $5,000–a vast sum in those days–but he never recovered a cent.

Being acutely aware of my responsibility, and that I knew little of machinery, I went through the factory with Metan, asking for explanation of the operation of the various units. I can particularly remember asking him, "What is that?"

"It is a steam trap," Metan replied.

"What does it do?" I asked.

"I don't know," he replied, "but I know the still can't work without it."

I said, "What if it breaks down during the crop? We'd better open it up and try to figure out how it works."

We did, and with the physics I had learned at school, we were able to figure out how it worked. Thank goodness it never gave any trouble, but I had to figure out how the steam pumps worked.

Fortunately I had studied Heat, Light and Sound at Emmanuel School, and Dynamics and Hydrostatics (in Physics) at Bedford Modern School. So with this, the little mechanics I had learned from my father (as a small boy when I was his shadow and he tinkered with the cars in the afternoon), and Metan at my side, I set out to learn all I could about the items of machinery that had been left in my care, but I don't think I ever figured out how the injector worked!

Paul had found most of the hillsides at Craigston pretty bare, as they were given out to the workers on the *métairie* system. The tenants grew corn, peas and cotton on these lands and were required to keep any lime trees thereon clean. The corn and peas they kept, but one-third of the cotton crop went to the Estate in lieu of rent.

They were also given an allowance of one penny per lime tree per annum. The erosion was tremendous and I have seen the water crossing Water Road about a foot deep and more than 100' wide. The water just swept down through the valley in a sheet. Paul, who was a very tidy and meticulous chap, dug a drain in 1938 from Water Road to the salt pond by the factory. That was the year of torrential rains (that swept away the Green Bridge near Queens Park in St. George's) and by the end of the rainy season, that drain was about 10' wide and 4' deep, and continued to erode year by year, until Paul, and then I, built concrete walls across them to stop further erosion, but that ravine is now about 20' wide and 10' at its deepest point.

Paul adopted the strategy of persuading the tenants to take gardens on the flat, and not giving any more new gardens on the hillsides, and letting those erstwhile gardens be covered in whatever vegetation volunteered. I continued this policy and at first there were just weeds, then bush, then indigenous trees, such as wild tamarind, cutlet and logwood emerged and over the years the trees have grown to form forests, and the run off, even after the heaviest rain, is minimal. Paul had started digging a ditch 10' long by 2' wide by 18" deep over the topside of every lime tree to conserve the rain. I got very interested in soil and water conservation, and later I contour-drained most of the fields and saw the volume of flood water diminish year by year.

The lime harvest generally started about October and ran through until about February, depending upon the rainfall, except in 1943 when we started the crop in October and ran right through the following year, until February of the subsequent year, and made a record crop harvest.

At that time Craigston employed anywhere up to seventy men cutlassing and draining and nearly one hundred women and girls, harvesting the limes. Mr. Stafford, a tall stately gentleman from Bogles, was in charge of the lime gang, and had been for many years. It was imperative that every field should be harvested at least once a week, otherwise the limes would rot. Sometimes the gang was split into two, but this was seldom. It was difficult to control these large gangs, as the "girls" always wanted to go where the limes were more plentiful. Sometimes there were more limes rotting on the ground than they could harvest. In those days they were paid by weight, so they soon discovered that green limes seemed to weigh more than ripe limes, and they preferred to pick the limes rather than to gather the ripe limes off the ground. This was frowned upon, particularly when the crop was in full-force, when it was forbidden.

During the peak of the crop, every available female was employed, but it was often difficult to get right 'round the fields in a week. If this was not done, some limes would rot. When they thought they had enough to fill a bag, they would fill one, then get skin from either the black sage or clammy cherry tree with which to sew the bags. By the time they had done this, their *blood run cold*, as they said, and it was difficult to persuade them to gather more. After Mr. Stafford died, I employed a series of male supervisors, but there were numerous complaints that they all favoured the prettier girls. I changed supervisors several times but the complaints continued, so one morning before they went out, I told them that I had tired of the complaints so I was giving them ten minutes to choose one from amongst themselves to be the supervisor. They chose Miss Baby Simon, who remained as supervisor to the end.

When I took over the management of Dumfries in 1943, I found that they had a different system, by which the limes were measured in the field in boxes that held one-third of a barrel (approximately 53 lbs.). With the boxes, Miss Baby was measuring all morning and the "girls" then knew all along how much they had earned, and instead of gathering three or four boxes for the day, they would gather six or seven. This method was much more satisfactory for everybody.

I was told that when they had payday in Craigston, the whole of Carriacou benefited, e.g., shopkeepers sold more goods, fishermen sold all their fish. But even before my time, Hankeys would send a big wooden box up with the pay, and the oxcart would be reversed on the jetty, and this box with shillings, sixpenny bits and coppers, would be labouriously hauled by the oxen up to Craigston for the pay, every fortnight.

When I joined, Craigston had a Model A Ford truck of ancient vintage, whose main function was to bring in limes during the crop harvest, and some 200 to 250 cords of firewood from Anse La Roche, out of crop. There was a small quantity of lime trees at Grand Bay Estate–run by Cephus Silvester, the overseer–and the truck hauled limes from Grand Bay every Thursday during the crop. Metan would leave for Grand Bay with the truck and a boy after lunch on Thursday, and usually return about 3:00 to 3:30 p.m. On one occasion he failed to return until about 5:00 p.m., and told me that he had had a tyre puncture in Limlair. He had no jack, but did have a wheel-spanner, so he cut down a small tree and with the aid of a stone and this lever, he lifted the truck sufficiently to put a stone under the axle, remove the wheel and roll it all the way to Craigston. By the time he had extracted the tube and vulcanised it, it was getting dark, so I told him to leave it until morning. He protested that he did not want to leave the truck on the road overnight, as someone might interfere with it. In spite of my protests, he rolled the wheel back up over Cherry Hill and down to Limlair and brought the truck in about 8:00 p.m. I think the truck did not have lights, so it was fortunate that there was moonlight.

On an occasion when Metan was bringing down a load of firewood from Anse La Roche, at a hairpin turn in Prospect a piece of wood slid through the slit in the back of the cab and went through the steering wheel to the floor. Metan was unable to turn the wheel to negotiate the bend, so the truck with him and the two footmen went plunging into the deep ravine that bordered the road. When I visited the scene, I could barely see the truck through the bushes from the road. That truck was essential to the harvesting of the crop! Fortunately it was still on four wheels and no one was injured. Next morning I asked Mr. Munro to go with Metan and a gang to start extracting it, while I sent off the various gangs, got the crushing going and made sure that all was well in the distillery. When I was going to Prospect at 9:00 a.m., I was amazed to see the truck being driven toward me.

I never quite discovered how they got it out of the ravine, but I remember Sandow Glean, the previous mechanic, telling me that when he was driving it to Grand Bay to collect limes and the brakes were defective, he changed into reverse gear over Top Hill and slipped the clutch all the way to Mount Pleasant. Those Model A trucks were rugged! Ours was the only truck available; there wasn't another to be begged, borrowed or stolen in case of a breakdown, so it had to be kept going at all costs. During the war when there were no parts to be had, Metan and I had to improvise. We couldn't get the belt that ran the water pump. We could run the truck without the generator, but not without the water pump. We improvised belts out of rope, leather and old tyres, and disconnected the starting motor. The truck could only then be started by manpower (pushing) or by gravity (run off). We learned to use every slope for starting. This meant that the battery was not being charged, but as it was used for ignition only, it lasted for several days, but then had to be taken to Joseph Bros. in Hillsborough, who would recharge it at XCD $2–a vast sum when men worked for one shilling per day, and women worked for 1p.

There was an occasion in the middle of a crop when the truck developed a miss. We did everything we knew such as changing oil, condenser, plugs and plug leads, but all to no avail. For more than a week I would go down at dawn to work on it until seven o'clock, or until I was required elsewhere. Having eliminated many possible faults in the ignition we turned to the mechanism and found that a piece had broken off a short plunger that activated a push rod to open a valve. We found an old engine rusting away, exchanged the part, installed it and the old truck was (almost) purring once more.

The truck would go out with Metan or me driving, and two footmen to collect bags of limes from the fields. These were jute sugar bags that held about 230 lbs. of limes, and in my early days, there was a good-natured competition to see who could back up to the truck, take one of these bags into the factory on their back and deposit it on the scale. Then the limes were weighed and stacked. The mill was an old cane mill with rollers driven by the Petter 6hp diesel engine. The bags of limes were emptied into a wooden hopper, run through the mill, the skins were spat out onto the floor, shovelled and taken out of the factory by wheelbarrow and dumped. The juice ran down into a large strainer where two lads sieved it, and the seed was taken out and dumped in the pastures nearby, where hundreds of doves feasted on it each day. The juice was then pumped up by brass hand-pump into a wooden trough which ran in the ceiling the whole way along, to two or three wooden vats in the sunken area next to the still. These vats were imported from Guyana, and were of greenheart bottoms with wallaba staves, and held together by iron-rod hoops, with a special device through which they ran, and where they could be tightened.

The standard bag of limes was 160 lbs., this when crushed, produced about 8 ½ imperial gallons of lime juice, which when distilled, would produce about 8 oz. of lime oil. At the time, we were never quite sure what lime oil was used for, but I later learned that lime oil was increasingly being used in preparation of men's toilet lotions and later, when Rose's was bought out by Cadbury-Schweppes, in the manufacture of Canada Dry Ginger Ale. It was shipped in special tins that Hankeys supplied, which were lined with a special substance because the lime oil was corrosive. After the small metal bungs were tightened down, a metal cap had to be soldered over it to prevent leakage. These were shipped to Hankeys in Grenada, who shipped them on consignment to Hankeys in London, and in due course an Account of Sale would be sent back to Grenada, showing the proceeds of the sale and all the incidental expenses charged. Presumably these were sent to my father in St. Patrick's, Grenada, but I was never privileged to see the results of my labour. Judging by the one sent to the previous owner, (dated 3rd February, 1920, when they shipped 653 casks of lime juice which yielded a net profit of £6 10s 4p) the reward for all the hard work was inconsiderable.

The crop harvest started in October and it would often be around Christmastime that sufficient lime juice had been collected to warrant starting the distillation. The boiler (a Morris boiler manufactured in Derby, England) was fuelled by firewood purchased from Anse la Roche Estate.

Anse la Roche was owned by a gentleman of uncertain temper called Mr. P.J. Sylvester. Legend has it that Mr. Sylvester's father, who owned the estate, sent him to Combermere School in Barbados. When he returned to Carriacou, he was put as a deckhand hauling firewood to Barbados (when I went to St. Lucia in 1957, I was told that St. Lucia had been exported to Barbados in the form of firewood and coals, and I suppose the same could be said for Carriacou). Mr. Sylvester would sit on the deck of his father's vessel and see his erstwhile schoolmates passing in their carriages. He developed a tremendous inferiority complex that was reflected in his demeanor and he had to be handled with great delicacy.

On one occasion he wrote me a very rude letter. I jumped on my motorcycle and sped to Anse La Roche. I found him picking cotton in a field with three women. I stormed into the field and demanded, "Do you mean to say that you wrote this letter to me, Mr. Sylvester?"

He replied, "A letter can be directed to anybody to whom it is addressed."

I realized that he would never admit fault, so I swung on my heel and was leaving the field when he shouted, "You went to school in England, I went to school in Barbados! You don't have more sense than me!

It was a peculiar arrangement by which the supply of firewood had to be made with Mr. Sylvester. I had to arrange with the woodcutters and submit the list of names to Mr. Sylvester for his approval. When this had been obtained and a contract for 50 or 100 cords of wood agreed upon, the cutters would cut, but Mr. Sylvester had to inspect each cord of wood (4' x 4' x 8') and mark it with a small twig or branch before Craigston was permitted to remove it. On only one occasion was this rule waived and that was when Mr. Sylvester fell ill in the middle of the contract and, to everyone's amazement, gave me permission to remove wood without his prior examination or his mark of approval. An unprecedented liberty!

We paid the woodcutters for the cutting, and paid Mr. Sylvester (10s per cord) for the wood. The wood was hauled down, one cord at a time, in the old Model A Ford truck to supply the fuel for the boiler. An enormous heap of wood would accumulate at the back of the lime factory, near to where the boiler is (but not too close!). It was always a tricky decision as to how much firewood to purchase. If too much was purchased, it would be consumed by termites or stolen before the next crop. If too little, there would not be enough fuel for the boiler and juice would have to be discarded, and limes left to rot. When my father bought Craigston there were blocks and blocks of paraffin wax, which was used for lining casks. In 1938 when there were unusually heavy rains resulting in an unusually heavy lime crop, Paul (who was manager at the time) ran out of wood, and paraffin blocks were burned in the boiler to keep the distillation going.

On one occasion when we had contracted for the purchase of 100 cords of wood but had only taken 25, Mr. Sylvester wrote a rude letter to me about one of the cutters who worked under his direction, but who was paid by Craigston. An exchange of letters ensued which led to my terminating the contract and paying the cutters for wood cut, and paying Mr. Sylvester for the 25 cords already supplied. In due course, he rode into Craigston yard one Sunday, mounted on a saddled donkey. I went out, greeted him civilly and invited him in to hold discussion. The outcome was that we agreed to resume the contract. When I had collected all 100 cords of wood, Mr. Sylvester asked for an account. Having paid him and the woodcutters for the initial 25 cords, I sent him an account for the remaining 75 cords and paid him for them. He wrote a sharp letter by return, in which he stated that my account was short and that, "... the shortage in your account was either the outcome of gross carelessness or a niggardly and willful act having an ugly aspect." I was astounded, but upon investigation found that he had questioned the cutters and, not knowing the initial 25 cords had been settled, gave him the total numbers they had cut. He added those up to 100 but neglected to deduct the 25 cords for which they had already been paid. Nonetheless, when the discrepancy had been explained and tempers had cooled, I resumed buying firewood from Mr. Sylvester, but he was always prickly.

Mr. Quammie stoked the boiler during the crop, and oversaw the pruning gang in the dry season. One time I visited a pruning gang of which Mr. Quammie was in charge. It was 2:00 p.m. and I found Mr. Quammie fast asleep under a tree, and I debated with myself. If I awoke him, discipline demanded that I should fire him, but as a boiler-man he was too valuable to me and to the estate to terminate his services, so I tiptoed away and pretended I hadn't seen him. I hadn't gone far when I heard the workers alerting him, saying, "The boss was here." I just kept going.

Mr. Quammie was an old hand at the game of stoking the boiler, but I could not understand why it was necessary to cram the boiler as full of wood as possible, so that in a short while, the safety valve would open and a lot of steam would escape (uselessly) then 20 minutes later the steam would be so low that we had to shut down the steam pumps, or even the still itself. I remonstrated with him, but with a voice of authority he told me that was how it had to work. One evening I sent Benton to get six bags, folded them, put them on top of a barrel as a cushion and asked Mr. Quammie to sit there and smoke his pipe while I fed the boiler. I half-filled the furnace with wood, then every five minutes I would open the door (the heat was intense!) and put in half-a-dozen pieces. Thereafter, the pressure remained at a fairly constant level, there was no more wastage of steam, and no shutdowns. When I had convinced myself that it could be done, I asked Mr. Quammie why it could not? He told me that he didn't know that that was how I wanted it fed!

There were two (later three) wooden vats with a capacity of 2,500-3,000 gallons each. As the citric acid in lime juice is highly corrosive, lime juice could only be stored in wood or in nonferrous metal containers (brass or copper). Not a BTU of steam could be wasted, so lime juice would be accumulated until the vats were nearly full. The decision to start distilling having been taken, Mr. Quammie would be instructed to, "get up steam" early on Monday morning. As soon as he had steam approaching 80 psi, he would telephone Craigston House and say, "Boss, I have up steam." I would immediately go down and pump juice from the vats to fill the steam-jacketed still, then fill the wash-heater's 500-gallon cylindrical tank. The hot vapours from the still passed through the wash-heater in a coil, preheating it so that the second distillation would take considerably less time for the extraction of all the oil. The jacket around the lower half of the still was supplied with steam from the boiler at low pressure; 8-9 psi. This caused the juice to boil and the condensing vapours then passed down through 144' of 2" copper piping which was cooled by the surrounding water, so that the condensate, water, and lime oil (a creamish liquid that looked like discoloured water) flowed out into the Florentine flask, where the precious oil was separated from the water. The water ran to waste. The Florentine flask was a copper container 16' wide x 2' deep with a copper partition in the middle that stopped short of the top. There was a valve at the bottom and a sight-glass on one side where the person monitoring the process could see just how much oil there was on top–in the half of the unit where the condensate fell and settled. This mixture of water and oil would rise as more liquid came in, and the trick was to watch this carefully, removing water from the bottom to ensure that water did not flow over the partition. When there was sufficient oil, the valve at the bottom was closed, and the oil and water rose until the oil flowed over the partition into the collecting chamber on the other side, where it was collected and then canned for export. Later I was to fit this with an inverted siphon so that the water ran off automatically and the liquid level remained constant.

The distillation continued uninterrupted until 8, 9 or 10 o'clock on a Saturday night. We always hoped the lime oil would stop flowing early, but we dare not afford to lose any. The operation of the still required great patience. When I think of how the distillation would go on for six days a week, 24 hours a day, with only a Tilley gas light, a hurricane lamp and a flashlight, I have to wonder! The staff required for this operation was Mr. Quammie (to feed the boiler), two boys (who hauled wood in to supply him), Miss Baby (who looked after the lime oil) and myself. I would be back and forth keeping a watch on the crushing, but making frequent trips to the distillery to ensure that steam pressure was being maintained at 80 psi, and that the water temperature in the condensing tank was kept cool. This was accomplished by pumping water from the two big tanks on the intermediate level to the bottom of the condensing tank and letting the warm water at the top overflow to the lower tank.

When I took over, the annual crop was about 2,500 lbs. of lime oil per annum, which, as a 160 lb. bag of limes yielded approximately 8 oz. of lime oil, represented 5,000 bags of limes. In 1943 we had a very good crop and produced 3,333 lbs. of lime oil, or nearly 7,000 bags of limes! The distillery was working 24 hours a day, six days a week for many weeks, and the water in the two bottom tanks became too warm to effectively cool the distillate. We made a trough 10' long x 5' wide with 4" sides; drilled hundreds of 1/4" holes in it so that overflowing water flowed into it and fell through the small holes, like a giant shower. This had the desired effect of cooling the water sufficiently so that the distillation could continue.

We were told by Hankeys that Craigston and Dumfries produced a very high quality lime oil and that they could always find a buyer on the London market. Nevertheless, they received only 30 shillings/lb. Shortly after the commencement of WWII, we were informed that the price of lime oil had risen to 70s/lb. on the London market. The Ministry of Food in England stepped in and controlled the price at 45s/lb. We were satisfied as it represented a 50% increase in price to us, and we considered that the other 25s/lb. was our contribution to the war effort as the lime oil went to America to help pay for lend-lease. We were told by Hankeys that each Caribbean producer was given a quota by the Ministry of Food in England, so could not ship until the quotas for the year had been released. An attempt was made by Caribbean producers to form a co-operative association for the marketing of lime oil, but this failed. So when the Ministry did deregulate it in the middle of 1945, some large producers sold at deflated prices, and those who tried to hold out for a better price only got 23s 6p/lb.

During this period, whenever repairs exceeded my capacity, I would send a telegram to Hankeys in St. George's, who would send up Mr. Zox Munro, a dear elderly gentleman who had no letters after his name, but had worked in factories in Canada. He had a vast experience and a knack for improvisation. He invariably stayed with me at Craigston House and in the evenings I would "pick his brain" and I learned a great deal from him.

On one occasion, when I was at Dumfries (which I managed from 1943) I had a telephone call that the boiler had "blown up." I rushed back as fast as my motorcycle would allow, with my heart in my mouth, as without a boiler, the remainder of the crop would be lost and this would have been a financial disaster. I found that the clever manufacturers of the boiler had inserted a white metal plug in the apex of the furnace, which was normally covered with water and remained solid, but the intent was that if the water level fell and exposed it, it would melt, condensation from the steam would gush down and put out the fire. This had happened!

Mr. Munro arrived by the next sailing boat and soon deduced that a one-inch galvanized-iron plug fitted. We had ingots of tin and lead, a crucible and a large blowlamp. Mr. Munro made a mixture of sand and clay, moistened it and rammed it into a small box surrounding a one-inch pipe-plug. With great patience, he then carefully unscrewed the plug, leaving a threaded hole into which he poured a mixture of molten tin and lead. When this had cooled, he extracted it, and spent hours cleaning the threads with a hacksaw. He then screwed it into the boiler and we anxiously filled the boiler with water and lit the fire. It worked perfectly, thereby saving our bacon.

With limes coming in at the rate of 300 or 400 bags per day at the peak of the crop, it was essential to make space in the storage vats for

2,000-3,000 gallons of fresh juice each day. In an attempt to cut down heat loss from the still, I ordered lagging material from Barbados (via Hankeys). This was a white clay-like substance which we mixed with coconut fibre and applied to all the copper surfaces to retain heat. Metan and I conspired to do all this lagging, but halfway through, it became evident that we did not have enough of the lagging material. Metan told me that similar material could be obtained from a cave in the hill above Steward Field. He went and brought a pail, and it looked remarkably similar, and with it we finished the job. The result was rewarding because we cut the time for the distillation of a 500-gallon batch by about an hour–thus saving 25% on the expenditure of wood.

In a further attempt to cut the time, and thereby the cost, Metan and I conspired to move the copper pipe through which the hot vapours ascended to the wash-heater, and slope it down from the top of the still, so that any vapours that condensed in it would flow out, and not back into the boiling juice. We extracted the condensing coil from the cooling tank, turned the pipe around and connected it so that the liquid would flow down and out. Having built the necessary platform etc., we erected the coil and built a concrete tank around it. Unhappily, we took advice that a proportion of burnt lime could be substituted for cement–which was relatively expensive–and there was no reinforcing steel available. This proved disastrous, because when completed, and we thought it was cured, I started pumping water into it with the steam pump. The water had risen to about 6' when I heard a loud explosion and rushed 'round the side of the still to be confronted by a 2' wall of water bearing down on me. I hastily retreated and climbed a wall and watched it–and my hopes–flow out to the sea! When the tidal wave had subsided, I went 'round to find a misshapen, tangled mess of copper pipes. I was shattered because our whole annual income depended upon being able to extract the oil.

With the help of Metan and Mr. Quammie, with blowlamp, chain, block and tackle, and using the posts in the factory as anchors, we were able to heat the bent pipes and return them (approximately) to their original shape. It was with great relief that we got everything back where it had been, and the distillation process going again. I never had the temerity to indulge in any further engineering feats!

During the dry season there was little field activity, except for a few of the men, who stayed to work as woodcutters on Mr. Sylvester's Anse la Roche Estate, the majority of the men would go off to Trinidad to work on the cane estates and there was little work for the women. But soon after the first rain fell, the men would return from Trinidad. For the first few weeks they would plant and weed their gardens, and then they would report back for work. Craigston was the only place offering employment of any scale.

At one time I planted up several acres of pigeon peas just so as to give the lime pickers work out of season. Unfortunately, we had an invasion of bad-jack ants. We had no effective insecticides, so we fought them with very primitive tools and it proved very unprofitable. My predecessor, Mr. Archer, tried collecting conger-eels to put them on trees to eat the blight.

On 3rd March, 1943, Mr. Haydock died and Hankeys offered me the job as manager of the Dumfries group of estates (Dumfries, Lauriston, Breteche and Sabazan) at a salary of XCD $80 per month. I jumped at it but did not have the temerity to ask for a travelling allowance. Mr. Haydock had been ill for some time with cancer and had made several trips to Grenada. During his absence I would liaise with Mr. Lucas Mends (the overseer) to keep things moving smoothly and pay the workers every fortnight. This I did *gratis* for Mr. Haydock. I was shocked when Hankeys instructed me to pay Mrs. Haydock 3/31 of Mr. Haydock's monthly salary (£30). They said that they would deal with Mrs. Haydock directly in Grenada. So I had the task of helping her and her children pack up their belongings (Mr. Haydock had lived there for 26 years) and ship them to Grenada or otherwise dispose of them. Reluctantly I took their bull terrier dog . . . remembering my father's admonition, "Never take a dog that's more than eight weeks old." That led to more drama, but that was later.

I would visit the Dumfries Group twice a week, on horseback or by motorcycle, and since it took quite a while to get there by horse, I would often stay until 1:00 p.m. or 2:00 p.m. I set out to contour-drain the cultivation at both Dumfries and Lauriston, so spent long hours in the hot sun laying out contour drains with a Bostrom level. I also set out to have ditches dug on the topside of every lime tree to conserve water runoff. I found that the old cane mill at Dumfries was so worn that it was only extracting about 7 oz. (of a possible maximum of 8.5 oz.) of lime oil from a 160 lb. bag of limes. I appealed to Hankeys for a new mill but was told that the estate couldn't afford a new one. I couldn't bear the thought of the lime oil that went to waste each year because of poor extraction, so set-to with hacksaw, cold-chisel, hammer, and my two bare hands.

Jean and I on our wedding day

Carriacou
in the 40s
(Management, Marriage, War)

When I came to Carriacou in January of 1940, I experienced a period of acute loneliness. I joined the Carriacou Sports and Social Club, and (during the season) would dash down soon after four o'clock to meet Mr. Harford Mendes, who was the wireless operator. Mr. Mendes had been the wireless operator from the days of signalling by heliograph (using a flashing mirror) and then Morse Code. A heliograph was signalled to the Police Station in St. Patrick's, users were required to submit their telegrams to the Revenue Office and pay 1s for 10 words.

He walked from Hillsborough to Belair and walked home every evening at four o'clock. He lived in town (near the present-day site of the Carriacou Museum) and he and I would carry out the coir matting and return for pads, bats, stumps and balls, and set everything up. If we did not, there would be no cricket. When at or about 5:30 p.m. when the batsman hooked a ball toward the boundary and your eyes travelled to see the fielder take the catch, you would be astounded to see that there was no fielder–he had just taken the shortcut through the bush home to Top Hill. But we had quite a lot of fun, and challenged one or two visiting teams from Grenada, and on one occasion, I took a team across to Ashton, on Union Island to play against the Union Island team.

A small group comprising Mr. Mendes, Mrs. Haydock, Cynthia Layne (the priest's wife), Dr. Commissiong and his wife, and I, played tennis twice a week and the Social Club met in St. Michael's Hall on Saturday evenings. There was table tennis, and card tables where different groups played bridge, canasta, all fours or dominoes. Members brought old magazines, so there was a reading section. There was no bar, but if a rubber of bridge dragged on, the participants would send out to the shop next door (Joseph Bros.) where a small flask of rum could be bought–also a tray of ice for 1s–but there was no heavy drinking. The membership consisted mainly of the clerks in the Government offices (all Grenadians) and the nurses (all Grenadians) and the tennis group. Someone suggested that the club should be enlarged and that each member should recruit two new members. Unfortunately, this brought in some rowdy elements who brought with them white rum and bad language, and the nurses were the first to withdraw, and in no time the club had burst.

On one of my infrequent trips (two or three times per year) to Grenada, I met a young lady named Jean Mancini, whose father was an electrical engineer, and whose mother was a Peterkin. In due course she consented to marry me, and on 18th November, 1943 we were wed in St. Patrick's Anglican Church in Grenada, by Canon

Gough. The reception was at Morne Fendue and we honeymooned at Green Island, being ferried over by the caretaker, David Swan, and one assistant. A week later we embarked on the weekly schooner and took up residence at Craigston.

It was a very spartan existence, as we had no stove, cooking was done on coal pots. It was a great occasion when Daddy bought a second-hand Electrolux fridge and sent it up. It absorbed my life for weeks, turning it upside down and changing baffles, changing kerosene and trimming wicks, but it never did more than produce cold water. In my bachelor days, water was pumped from the large cistern by a brass hand-pump to a tank on the platform at the back, whence it was taken by pail to supply the kitchen and the ewers (large jugs that stood by the china basins on the wash-stands in the bedrooms). In preparation for my bride, I had built a concrete block building on the platform at the back that housed a shower and a water closet–I think the first ever on Carriacou. On top, I built a shallow holding tank which supplied them, and also supplied water to the bedrooms.

Our life was austere, but we had settled into the routine of Carriacou: From time to time we had friends or relatives visit and would take them exploring or to picnic on Petit St. Vincent or Sandy Island. We did have an RCA Victor radio, run off a 12v battery, which was kept charged by a wind-charger that my brother Paul had erected. This was used mainly to listen to war news from BBC. On Saturday nights, we could also get special programmes on an American station from Connecticut. There were no local stations to tap into. Our social life in the early days consisted of having the Anglican priest (Father Pipe) to dinner every Sunday night, and the Catholic priest (Father Devas) to dinner every Wednesday night, and occasionally, the Commissioner (Mr. Knight) to dinner on a Thursday . . . but never together. As Jean was an excellent cook and we separated milk (as Mother had done) and made our own fresh cream and butter, and collected wild cherries and guavas, she could always give them a meal, something they all looked forward to for the whole week. Occasionally, we would have the nurses from the hospital over to play canasta.

We had the Pontiac car which was then 14-years-old, Daddy having used it in Grenada for some 12 years before sending it to Carriacou. I have a vivid recollection of a car being landed off a schooner on the beach at Hillsborough, which could only be done when the sea was calm, as two fishing boats were lashed together and planked with heavy lumber. They were tied to the schooner while the car was lifted by block-and-tackle, and dropped over the side onto the planked boats. These were then hauled inshore and brought to the surf broadside on, and planks were laid to the beach. Many hands pulled and pushed the car onto the beach, and up onto the sand road–all roads being sand. Because there were very few trees, on a moonlit night the roads stood out like white ribbons.

With the war on in Europe and the East, imported foodstuffs were in very short supply. We had to subsist on fish, the odd chicken raised in the yard, or lamb or goat purchased from the Fish & Flesh House early on Saturday mornings. Beef was only available on special occasions, as too often the butcher had seen his customers turn to the beach when boatloads of jacks arrived from Canouan or Mayreau, and as there was no refrigeration, his beef would have to be dumped. In periods of drought, when stored corn and peas had been consumed, there was a great dependency on bananas, bluggoes, breadfruit and coconuts from Grenada. Traditionally, two or three sailing sloops would leave Hillsborough on a Monday morning for St. George's, and would return on Thursday or Friday, depending on the vagaries of wind and tide. As breadfruit ripens quickly, they had to be roasted before shipment. The housewives would stream down to Hillsborough with their baskets on Thursdays, and often spend the whole day with their eyes glued on Point Cistern, hoping to see a sail appear, then trudge home disappointed in the evening. Even when the boats did appear, there were seldom sufficient supplies to satisfy everyone. I was told by such a housewife that she had only gotten three ripe bananas, and as she and her husband had four children, they each had half a banana. To find a tin of corned beef or condensed milk in a shop was a rare treat. Very infrequently, the firm of W.E. Julien & Co. would get in a few bags of flour. I explained to the manager that my 90-odd workers were earning a living, and could not spend day after day in Hillsborough, so if he would trust me with a bag of flour, I would sell one pound to each worker. This entailed buying bags, weighing out the flour for the estate workers, and sometimes ending up with half-a-pound for ourselves.

On one occasion I returned from meeting the mail boat to tell Jean that I had met a nice American couple, The Pembertons, and had invited them to dinner. "Dinner?" she queried, "What on earth are we going to give them to eat?" I had not given the matter any thought, but I quickly said, "Oh, I will go to the swamp and see if I can get a duck." The duck in question, being the green-winged teal and blue-winged teal that flew down from North America every winter. They abounded in the Lauriston swamp, but were difficult to find between the mangrove clumps. I took my shotgun, filled my pockets with shells, and went down shortly before dusk. As I entered the swamp, I saw a single duck cruising along, but it was a long way off. There was a low bush between me and it, so I got down on hands and knees in about 8" of water and crawled nearer. As I slowly raised my gun, another duck came swimming into view, and I thought, "Well, if I can get two ducks with one shot–I knew there would not be a second chance–we can each have a portion of duck, and then afters!" But they were wary birds, and refused to get into line! I had just decided that discretion was the better part of valour and as I fired, two ducks crossed and I was amazed to see about 100 ducks or more that I had not seen, rise out of the swamp and bunch, as they always did. I rushed in and was surprised to gather four ducks, so was able to provide my wife with meat for the table.

It must have been somewhere about 1944 that Jean's sister Celia, both of her parents having died in St. Andrew's, came to live with us for about a year. Somehow it was arranged for her to go on to stay with the Chapmans in Barbados (friends of her parents). Jean's brother Keith Mancini, who had been the overseer at Waltham Estate in St. Mark's, volunteered for the Canadian Armed Forces and together with a bunch of other young men (Leo DeGale, Mike Bain, Colin Ross) left for Canada. Keith's manager, Mr. Ralph Alexander (a cavalryman in WWI) kept the job open and paid his salary for the duration of his absence. When he returned–he had been a spotter with a Canadian Artillery Regiment–he was slightly shell-shocked and spent several weeks with us on Carriacou, before resuming his duties at Waltham Estate.

I had a one-third share, with Gordon Gentle and Eric Copland, in a double-ended whaling boat from Bequia which we named *Typhoon*. Gordon found an old Model A Ford engine under a breadfruit tree in St. Andrew's, bought it for XCD $80 and Colin McIntyre installed it, complete with gear lever, clutch, brake. My heart was always in my mouth when I had women and children (or priests!) onboard, but it never did fail. On an occasion, the Catholic priest, Father Devas (who was a great ornithologist and had written a book on birds of Grenada) asked that I take him to The Sisters. He told me that a red-billed tropicbird had been seen off The Sisters–two rocks that lay off the entrance to Hillsborough Bay. He asked if I would take him to look for it, and I did. As we circled the rock, I was tending to a trolling line when I heard a loud shout and looked up expecting to find that we were running aground, but found Father Devas standing with both arms extended in the air, shouting, "I've seen it! I've seen it! Thank God, I've seen it! The red-billed tropicbird!" He was elated and I was in need of brandy.

The doctors had always been personal friends of ours, but we had a new doctor on Carriacou whom we had not gotten to know socially. Jean was expecting our first child and kept in very good health during her pregnancy. As the mail service was provided by sailing sloops (the schooners with engines had been diverted to ferrying goods from Barbados and Trinidad) from about six weeks prior to Jean's due-date we were on the lookout for such a schooner.

From time to time, one of these would pass in, but none did. A large sloop had been launched from near the Catholic Church, and rode at anchor for many weeks, as the owners gathered rigging, sails, etc. I heard that she was going to Grenada (on her maiden voyage) to be registered. I approached one of the owners and was told that she was going on Monday and we must be onboard by 4:00 p.m. Jean and I boarded with a deckchair, a flask of coffee and some sandwiches (there were no cabin accommodations). By 5:00 p.m. a boy and a man, who claimed to be the mate, rowed out and came aboard. The mate's first reaction was, "Oh Gad! De boom break!" Indeed, the boom consisted of two pieces of round wood, spliced and drummed and supported by a topping lift. This had gone slack and the boom had sunk onto the cabin top. "Boy!" the mate called, "Bring me some rope!"

"Please Sah! It don 'ave no rope!" was the reply.

"What?! 'Ow you could 'ave a vessel widout rope?"

A short while later it was, "Boy! Bring me a 'ammer an' some nails!"

"Please Sah! It don 'ave no 'ammer!"

"What?! 'Ow you could 'ave a vessel widout 'ammer? Well bring some nails!"

"Please Sah! It don 'ave no nails!"

"What?! Better they sell the vessel and buy some parts!"

This was amusing but not very reassuring so when at about 8:00 p.m. the crew came aboard (drunk), we seriously considered going ashore, but I did not relish the thought of being midwife! The weather was calm–it was brilliantly moonlit–so we decided to stick it out. It was after 9:00 p.m. when we set sail and were between Isle de Ronde and Sauteurs at one o'clock in the morning, when I saw a big black squall coming down from Petite Martinique. I said to the captain that I didn't like the look of it–I thought it had a lot of wind in it–so I suggested to him that he shorten sail. He shouted for the crew to come up from the fo'c's'le, but when they did, they asked him angrily why he had called them? He told them, "Because of the approaching squall." They said, "That stupid likkle squall, you wake up a man for?" and grumbling, returned below. Twenty minutes later the squall hit us, the boat heeled over, the boom went into the sea and really broke this time. With the weight of the canvas in the water, the boat listed alarmingly, and Jean and deckchair, and I clutching onto it, slid across into a foot of water on the lee side. Only the railing stopped us from sliding off into the sea. This time the crew did rush up and cut away the broken boom and part of the sail, and the boat righted itself. We sailed on, but at 8:00 a.m. we were becalmed off Beausejour (on the west coast of Grenada). I asked the captain to put us ashore and he had us rowed in. We walked about a mile to the nearest telephone and called Colin McIntyre, who kindly sent a car from St. George's to collect us. Taxis were not readily available at this time. We stayed with the Zox Munros in Scott Street, and the next morning walked up to the hospital, where Jean presented herself to the house physician (an Englishman). He bridled and said, "I can't take your case, I haven't seen you at all during your pregnancy. Who is your doctor?" When she told him that she had not seen a doctor during her pregnancy, he was appalled. That night Jean had Trevor.

Six weeks later, I was bringing Jean and Trevor up in *Typhoon,* and off Isle de Ronde, we had engine trouble, but Jean was adamant that we should not turn back as we would only have to face the trip again next day. I found the problem, and we came on to Carriacou. Wet, but glad to have the journey behind us.

German submarines were very active in the area and the steamships that supplied the islands only came in convoy to St. Lucia, Barbados and Trinidad. Everything that came to the smaller islands was transhipped by schooner. One evening about seven o'clock, one of the Miss Forteaus (who manned the telephone exchange) called to ask if I had heard of the lifeboat with survivors that had come in. They were housed at Mr. Cropper's Guest House, the only one on the island. I took some fruit and half of a roasted chicken, which was all that we had, and went to visit them. There I met nine Norwegian sailors whose ship had been torpedoed to the northeast of Barbados. I was surprised when the chief officer offered me a cigar. He then told me the following story:

He said that an area off Barbados was known as "Torpedo Alley" as so many ships had been sunk there. On the evening of the sinking of his ship, he had been on watch and at 11:40 p.m. he had seen a torpedo pass 50' in front of their ship. He called up the captain, who had been asleep, and he was not impressed. The captain said it must have been a flying-fish! The officer went off duty at midnight convinced that it had been a torpedo, so he went to his cabin, put on suitable clothes, packed a small suitcase with things he wished to save, and as there was a little space, he put in a box of cigars. At 12:20 a.m. a torpedo struck. They had with them a sailor who had been standing on deck above where the torpedo struck and whose feet were badly burnt. He was in the Princess Royal Hospital, but next day the commissioner sent them off in their lifeboat (with a guide) to St. George's where the injured sailor could get better medical attention.

The stuff that floated ashore on the beaches was just amazing; drums of peanut oil, quantities of raw rubber, shoes, even some bags of flour. I never saw these items but was told that the flour on the outside caked, forming a casing inside the bag and the flour at the centre would be perfectly dry. All flotsam was supposed to be reported to the government, but this was "honoured in the breach." Drums of peanut oil disappeared into kitchens or the bush, and being continuously open and exposed to air, soon went rancid. The smell of rancid oil being used for cooking soon displaced the sweet scents around the island.

Late in 1944 a mine washed up on the beach at Windward overnight. A man going early in the day to move his goats saw it in the gentle surf, floated it out and pushed it up to his property where he rolled it up the beach and covered it with some coconut branches. A fisherman–always on the lookout for the tracks of turtles that may have come ashore to lay eggs–saw the marks, followed them to the mine, rolled it back into the sea and floated it down to his property, where he secured it. A short while before, an American motor torpedo boat, ordered from the base in Trinidad to the base at Vieux Fort, St. Lucia, had struck a reef to the east of Petite Martinique, and the villagers seemed to be convinced that the crew had stuffed all the gold and dollars they had into this sphere and thrown it overboard, to save it. Some Barbadian masons, who were working on a house about a hundred metres away, told them that it was a mine, but in spite of this warning, some boys kept going at it. When they rotated an arm attached to it the mine would start ticking. They would reverse the rotation and it would stop. For eight days they worried it. On the 9th day they went at it in earnest with cold-chisel and hammer and it exploded, killing nine people.

That afternoon, our baby's nurse came running up the driveway to say that the commissioner had passed by, and said that a mine had killed nine people in Windward, and I was to come! I did not understand why it should be me, but I put my shotgun and a box of cartridges in the car and drove over to Windward. I met a sad scene. The two lads who were at the mine were blown to pieces and mostly out to sea, and the bodies of the other seven lay strewn about. Two of the victims were small flaxen-haired girls who were collecting woodchips from near where a vessel was being built. Another was a shipwright who had a piece of shrapnel pass through his neck. There were of course no stretchers, but I suggested that the villagers unhinge some doors on which to carry the victims home. This they did.

A few months later, another such mine floated ashore onto a sandbank off Windward, but this time the villagers were more cautious, and reported it to the authorities. A British destroyer came and exploded it harmlessly. Shortly thereafter, there was an official enquiry, which I attended in Magistrate's Court House. There was a reluctance on the part of the villagers to give any evidence as they thought they might be blamed for having not reported the presence of the mine, but when a rumour was circulated that the British government might pay compensation to the families of the victims, the evidence poured in.

A few days after the incident of the first mine, Mr. Knight called to say a mine disposal squad of three men was coming from British Guyana by seaplane to investigate. He would take one in, the doctor would have one, would we have the other? Jean agreed so we did have one stay with us. He told me that this was one of several hundred French briquet mines that had been sown off the coast of Africa in 1940, and had broken loose and drifted across the Atlantic. Many of them had come ashore on the salt-flats of British Guyana, so he was familiar with them. He showed a picture to people in Windward, and they recognized it.

By 1949, after nine years of hard work, I was told by Hankeys that sufficient of the debt had been repaid to permit Morne Fendue to be removed from the mortgage they held on all of Daddy's real estate in Grenada and Carriacou–much to Mother's relief.

When I got married in 1943, my salary was raised from XCD $45 to $75 per month. Fortuitously, when Hankeys offered me the job at Dumfries following Mr. Haydock's death, my total salary was $155 per month. Jean and I had two children, Trevor and Diana, and a third child on the way (Peter). We could see little chance for advancement and the day would soon come when we would have to send the children to school in Grenada. Although the Kents owned four estates in Grenada (Plains, Chambord, Mt. Rich and Simon) there was little chance they could offer me employment so I applied to Mr. Walter DeGale, who owned Dumferline Estate and was attorney to several others. What a pleasant surprise when a letter arrived offering me the post of manager of Carriere Estate in Grenada at the princely sum of XCD $144 per month. Still! It would get my foot in the door of managing a cocoa estate in Grenada. I had been brought up on a cocoa estate but had been away six years in England and spent a decade on Carriacou and had not proven myself as a cocoa man, so I was glad of the opportunity to learn and perhaps show my worth.

In retrospect, I'm sure that had I asked Hankeys, my salaries would have been increased, as they had told me debts that had been on their books for years had been paid off.

cocoa pickers

Carriere
and General Strike of '51

I left Carriacou to take over the management of Carriere Estate on January 16, 1950, and introduced myself to the overseer, Mr. Lott Stanislaus. When Mr. Walter DeGale did not appear, I phoned him, only to be told, "Oh, I'm not coming, you take over." Fortunately, the overseer was a genial and friendly person, who accepted me without reservation.

An unfurnished house was provided but no transportation, so my family had taken refuge at Morne Fendue. Fortunately, my brother-in-law Keith Mancini, had agreed to sell me his Ford Prefect, so I was able to commute from Morne Fendue to Carriere until we got together enough furniture for the family to be able to move into the house which had three bedrooms, bathroom, living room, dining room, verandah and kitchen, but no electricity. Cooking was done on a wood stove and coal pots. It was a couple of years before Mr. DeGale decreed that the Estate should provide a kerosene stove and one drum of kerosene per month. This was a great leap forward. The detached garage was the old stable with some minor modifications. There was a storeroom and a room known as the "Servants' Room" attached to the kitchen. Every Friday the estate's tractor would unload large quantities of bluggoes, breadfruit, and occasionally, a bunch of bananas; enough to feed the family, servants, dogs, fowl and pigs for a week.

Carriere was a long narrow estate of some 250 acres, stretching from an elevation of about 150' to 1,100' above sea level. The lower portion of the estate had some scattered cocoa, but much of it had died out. The middle portion where the manager's and overseer's houses, office, and boucan were located had the bulk of the cultivation, and the upper portion had some cocoa and coconuts. There were windbreaks of enormous mango trees and breadfruit trees.

I reported to work at Carriere at 7:10 a.m. and thereafter during the seven years I managed Carriere that routine was maintained. We would hold a ten to fifteen minute consultation on work to be performed, and then punctually at 7:30 a.m. Mr. Stanislaus sent the ninety-six workers off to their allotted tasks. Two women gathered nutmegs and the other "task workers" were allotted tasks for drainers and cutlassers, and would generally finish their tasks and go home by 11:00 a.m., while pruners, men digging holes to plant cocoa or bananas, or women picking peas were on "day work" and had to be present from 7:30 a.m. to 4:00 p.m. with an hour's break for lunch. There were two watchmen and four drivers (as the foremen were called). These latter went out with the various gangs of workers each morning. They either measured the tasks and saw that the work was performed satisfactorily, or in the case of the cocoa pickers, that all ripe pods were harvested.

During the cocoa crop there were two gangs of pickers, each consisting of five men and five women. The men each had a steel cocoa knife attached to a slim bamboo rod about 8' to 10' long. The women each had a basket which they balanced on their heads and a cutlass with a sharp point. Cocoa pods have short (½" to 3/4") stems by which they are attached to the cushions on the stems and limbs of the cocoa trees. These cushions are small bumps on the skin of the trunk or limbs from which the flower–eventually the pods–emerge. It is important to not damage these cushions and it is amazing how a proficient picker will slice off a pod with an upward thrust of his knife and pick another with a downward pull. His partner follows with a basket on her head and impales a pod on the point of her cutlass, swings it up, taps the knife against the basket to dislodge the pod (which falls into the basket) and then goes for the next pod, all in one fluid motion. The pickers know that five full baskets of pods will net one basket of seed, so each assembles five heaps of pods where the given task is five baskets of seed (per pair). The picker then cuts some banana leaves and lays them on the ground, side by side, to make a surface on which he drops the cracked pods. These, he picks up with the point of a cutlass, holds it in his hand, cracks it with a sharp chop of the cutlass and drops it onto the leaves. His partner strips the seeds off the placenta into the basket. When this is full and mounded, it is emptied into a canvas bag for transport to the sweat boxes in the boucan.

The boucan workforce consisted of four elderly ladies and a boucan overseer, Mr. St. Bernard, a dear gentleman, absolutely trustworthy. He rode up every morning on a saddled donkey, very dignified. He saw to the preparation of cocoa and nutmegs for market, and weighed and recorded the prices of bluggoes and breadfruit sold to the workers each Wednesday and Saturday. This produce was harvested by the workers–under the supervision of the watchman–and sold at a nominal price of 4 lbs. of bluggoes for a penny, and 12 breadfruit for a penny.

Mr. St. Bernard and the boucan workers spread the fermented cocoa from the sweat boxes where it had been dumped by able-bodied women who had carried baskets of raw beans weighing 70 to 80 lbs. on their heads from the fields. The beans were fermented for seven or eight days, to convert the cotyledon in the beans to the hard chips with strong chocolate flavour. The fermenting wet beans soon produced very high temperatures, so that after two or three days a hand thrust into the centre would find the heat uncomfortable. The sweat boxes had removable panels to the front so that the beans could be transferred by strong men using wooden shovels, from one box to its neighbour–moving the beans which had been on the outside of the pile, to a more central position, thus ensuring that all beans received proper fermentation. When Mr. St. Bernard was satisfied that the beans had reached the optimum stage of fermentation, they were spread to dry–either on the two big drying floors covered by a large roof on wheels, or on drawers that nested under the roofs and were pulled out to expose the beans to full sunlight.

In 1954 the big estates were mortified when this upstart from Carriacou won "The Cup," but it was entirely due to Mr. St. Bernard. Every estate submitted an entry to the Grenada Agricultural Exhibition, and the prize was to win this silver cup engraved, "1st Prize for Best Fine Estate Cocoa." I was able to walk into "The Club" and announce, "I won The Cup, don't you know!" But I've always regretted not giving that cup to Mr. St. Bernard.

Mr. DeGale was attorney for my first year and signed cheques, but he never visited the estate. About two weeks after I arrived, he called to tell me that he and Management were going to Barbados for two weeks so, "Look after everything." My heart sank as now I had nobody to whom I could turn for advice. On his return Mr. DeGale called and asked, "Edward! How is everything going?" I told him that all was well. He replied, "I knew it would be!" What a boost that gave to my confidence. Although Mr. DeGale and my father were friends, he hardly knew me, as I spent six years in England and ten years on Carriacou. Indeed, later on he told me that the only reason he had given me the job was because my father "was such a fine sportsman." After a year Mr. DeGale resigned as attorney and appointed me in his place.

Initially I found that the workers were getting no more than a few days of work per week. The able-bodied men were getting three days of work, and the women and men who couldn't do heavy work, were getting but two days of work per week. So everybody was burning coals, or minding animals, or fishing, or had a little garden or whatever they could do to supplement their income.

I was appalled at the deplorable condition of the worker's housing and determined to do something about it. We had ninety-six workers, many of them living on the estate, and their housing was dreadful. Their homes were made of old salt-fish boxes or barrels and any little piece of galvanized iron, with a thatch roof of course, partitions made of sacking, parents on this side, children on that side; maybe they were all together, I don't know, but the conditions were dreadful.

I called the workers together and said, "Your houses are in a dreadful condition. If you will agree to do what I tell you, I will guarantee you five days of work per week, if you promise me that when you go into the field you will work. Do you agree? Do you promise me?" They said, "Yes," and I said, "Okay, from next week we're working five days a week. Everyone, men and women."

We had hundreds, if not thousands, of breadfruit trees on the estate and there were woodcutters who used these great two-man saws with a handle at each end. I remember that at the time sawn lumber was selling for XCD $17 per thousand board feet (that works out to only 1.7 cents a board foot!). So I told the workers that the estate would donate the trees for lumber. We lent them the money to purchase building material and sent the estate's tractor into Grenville to pick up the material–galvanized sheeting, nails, etc. After a year or two the standard of housing had improved greatly.

Which leads me to the tale of Mr. and Mrs. Trouble. That was their real name: Trouble. I called them in and said, "Mr. and Mrs. Trouble, your house is a disgrace to the estate. It right on the public road and everybody see it and they believe we not paying you, or we not giving you work." Now the thing was, Mr. Trouble would go to the rum shop on payday (he and his wife lived in one direction but he headed off in the other direction.) We paid every fortnight and he would drink or gamble away all his money and they lived on Mrs. Trouble's wages. So I said, "If you all will agree to giving me $2 each a fortnight, (which was quite a considerable sum because they were only getting a dollar or something per day) I will rebuild your house for you."

To my surprise Mr. Trouble said, "Yes boss, yes!"

"Are you sure?" I asked.

"Yes boss! Yes!"

When it was finished, the Troubles owed me about XCD $140. It was just a little house, about 10' x 14', but the way Mrs. Trouble kept it you would have believed it was Buckingham Palace . . . with a galvanized roof! She was so proud of her new house, she made little curtains and hung them in the window, she got a piece of poultry wire to protect the rose bush she planted by her front door, never mind that you had to step on a stone to get in.

At that time we had a system for producing pen manure for the cocoa field. During the dry season wherever there was an open space, one or more of the workers were allowed to keep *cow on pole*. The cow was tethered with a chain to a stake in the middle. In those days we didn't have cement bag straps, we used chain, perhaps 12' long. The workers could chop up the trunks of any bananas that were harvested and they could cut grass for feed, and the cow was kept on pole. In the dry season the estate would harvest the pen manure from these poles. The green stuff was removed from the top and the manure below was forked into baskets and headed by women to the cocoa field where it was dumped and subsequently covered over by the men.

So Mr. and Mrs. Trouble kept a cow on pole and once their pole had been harvested the gross came to $120. I called them in and said, "Mr. and Mrs. Trouble, you owe me $140 and the money from the pole come to $120. You worked very hard all year and I'm sure you want a little something for yourselves. Let's say I take $80 and I give you $40." And to my surprise, the first to say, "No boss, take all," was Mr. Trouble. I argued with him saying, "No, you work hard all year," but they both insisted, "No boss, take all." So I maybe took $70 and gave them $50. They continued to pay $2 every fortnight and eventually they paid back the balance in full.

Trade unionism in Grenada was in its infancy. On Carriacou it was nonexistent and good labour relations depended to a large degree on the standards and ethics of management. Paul and I maintained a high standard of honesty and fair play in dealing with the workers and I do not recall any disputes, other than the disciplinary action of "sending home" workers for a day or two. When I arrived at Carriere there was no trade union activity on the estate. I found that wages were fixed by agreements between the Grenada Agricultural Association (GAA) and a trade union based in Gouyave (GWU), which negotiated small increases in the agricultural wage from time to time.

I soon joined The GAA, an association of large and small landowners led by Sir Joseph De La Mothe, Chairman/President, with other very conservative landowners comprising the executive.

Eric Matthew Gairy had recently *burst on the scene,* returning from the oil refineries in Aruba where he had been engaged in trade union activity. He formed the Grenada Manual and Mental Workers Union (GMMWU) and had organized the sugar workers in the south of Grenada. I was present at a general meeting of the GAA (my first public meeting in Grenada) and listened with some surprise to the president advise the body that they had received a demand from the GMMWU for an increase of 10% on the wages paid to agricultural workers. The president explained that he had only recently heard of the GMMWU; that GAA was in the process of negotiating a new agreement with the GWU, so couldn't entertain this new demand.

This idea seemed to meet with general approval so I rose to ask, "How could the GAA refuse to negotiate with GMMWU if the union had demonstrated that it represented the majority of the workers?" While I was speaking, the president leaned aside to start a conversation with the secretary, Mr. Charlie Philips. I stopped speaking. The president looked up and saw me standing and he indicated that I should continue. This I did, but when he again leaned aside and it was plain to all that he was not paying attention, I stopped again. He looked up, asked me to continue and this time appeared to listen. But, he did not answer my question and it was apparent that the "Old Boys Network" was not about to heed the protest of a virtually unknown upstart from Carriacou.

It was as a result of this attitude that a group of younger planters with more liberal ideas, led by Denis Henry, formed the Grenada Agriculturists' Union (GAU). Denis Henry explained that under Grenada law, a union had rights and privileges denied to an association. The new agricultural union took up the cudgels on behalf of the landowners, and the GAA faded into obscurity. But not before the devastating strike of 1951....

The GMMWU had demanded an increase of 10% to the existing wage. The Grenada Workers Union (GWU) had requested an increase of one shilling per day. At the time the wage for able-bodied men (who dug drains, pruned, forked and picked cocoa) was 3s 6p per day. The increase took the GWU wage to 4s 6p per day, while the GMMWU demand would have increased the wage to only XCD 92.5 cents (approximately four shillings). The directorate of the Agricultural Association thought that by granting the demand of the GWU, they would also satisfy Mr. Gairy's demands, but of course Mr. Gairy was more interested in gaining recognition than getting an increase in wages. He called the general strike of agricultural workers that lasted six weeks and crippled the agricultural sector.

We had two watchmen on the estate. When the strike began, I asked Eldon, who was watchman on the upper part of the estate, to come down and occupy the other watchman's house near the boucan, and stay out of sight. On the first evening of the strike, a crowd of our workers congregated outside the main gate to the boucan compound. I walked casually down to the gate to investigate the cause of the agitation. The crowd declared that Eldon was turning the cocoa in the sweat boxes. Just when I thought I had persuaded them that Eldon was not working, a band of young men carrying sticks burst over the gate. Eldon fled to the overseer's house where he took refuge under the overseer's bed. Part of this band jumped over to my left and some to my right. I went running after the first group shouting, "You can't come in here like this!" but they just melted into the pasture. When I got back to the gate, I learned that Eldon had run to the overseer's house. I argued with a couple of the ring leaders that Eldon had not been working; we didn't want him to work, all we wanted was for him to go home unharmed. They agreed that they would not harm him, so I went up to the overseer's house and extricated Eldon from under the bed. We walked him down to the gate where a lot of our workers were still assembled, through the crowd and about 100 yards down the road to get him well away from the crowd (a couple of the ring leaders accompanied us). When we had gone what I adjudged to be far enough, I told Eldon to go home and not to come back until I sent for him. As we returned to the gate, there was a brief fracas down the road. We later learned that they had opened blows on Eldon, put a knife to his back and frogmarched him a few hundred yards toward his home before releasing him. I rushed up to my home to call the Grenville Police Station. They did not seem sympathetic and it soon became apparent that their sympathies were with the strikers. The sergeant and two policemen appeared two and a half hours later. By that time the crowd had dispersed and all was peaceful. I found out later that Eldon was not seriously hurt.

We were apprehensive the next day as a few groups of workers had patrolled the public road nearby, carrying cocoa knives and cutlasses, which they occasionally scraped on the road to make the most blood curdling sound.

Our house was situated a few hundred feet from the compound that contained the boucan, sweat boxes, drying floors and drawers, the office, the overseer's house and the watchman's house. The whole compound lay alongside the public road that ran from Moyah Bridge to St. John's Hill.

My first intimation of the strike was upon hearing a loudspeaker ordering the workers on the estate to stop work. At the time I was in the upper part of the estate. Fearing for my family's safety, I ran home as fast as I could. We had three young children and as we lived so close to the public road, it was impossible to keep them in the house all day, so Jean and I decided to take them over to my father's home at Morne Fendue which was two miles away and more isolated. I felt they would be safer since both my father and my sister were popular with the workers. So on the second day of the strike I drove them all over to Morne Fendue, and left them under the protection of my sister, Betty Mascoll. There were fond farewells, as no one knew what to expect next. On my return to Carriere, I found all was quiet.

I arranged with Mr. Stanislaus that he and his family would continue to spend the days in his house but come across and spend the nights in my house. He and I pulled out some of the drawers on which cocoa beans were drying, but we couldn't move the heavy roofs that needed to be rolled out to expose the beans to sunlight. We did what we could and no one threatened us.

Many of the workers did not really understand the implications of the strike and were as apprehensive as we were. Some of them asked what a strike was. It was so touching when the four ladies who worked in the boucan came to me on that first day of the strike and said, "Boss, we have no complaint. We don't know about this strike." I explained that *strike* did not mean *blows*, it just meant refusing to sell their labour to the estate for the wage offered. I thanked them but advised them to go home and stay there until I sent for them.

This apprehension was heightened by the stories of the homes of *blacklegs* (strike breakers; workers who continued to work during the strike) having their small houses mysteriously catch fire at night and burn to the ground. The policy was known as "Sky Red" and was effective in subduing those workers who held feelings of loyalty to their employers and had dared to work.

Mr. Gairy had led a march of striking sugar workers into St. George's, been arrested and conveyed on a British warship to Carriacou, but his lieutenants (Gascoigne, Blaize, RCP Moore) all kept the fires burning, and it was six weeks before the Agricultural Association capitulated to Gairy's demands and normal work was resumed on the estates.

Meanwhile, as management, Mr. Stanislaus and I determined to try to save the cocoa in the sweat boxes–which would surely rot if not removed.

One small room in my house was reserved for Mr. Stanislaus and his family. Every night before dark they moved across. We piled up all the furniture into one small room. Each morning I drove my Ford Prefect down to the sweat boxes. Mr. Stanislaus and I dug out as much of the fermenting cocoa as the car could carry. I drove it up to my house and we spread it throughout the house on the floor of bedrooms, dining room, living room and verandah. No one interfered, even though these trips entailed driving out onto the public road for 75 yards. We were kept pretty busy, as we also pulled out some of the drying drawers, so we had to keep an eye open for any approaching rain, when they had hastily to be pushed in. Every day Mr. Stanislaus and I would work diligently to expose beans to sunlight or stir them on the floors or drawers and at the end we were able to save nearly all of the produce in the boucan and surrounding buildings. Some of the cocoa mildewed, so it did not fetch top price, but not a pound rotted.

It was remarkable that although the surrounding estates had produce looted from their buildings, Carriere's buildings were not attacked. Much later we found that in those early days, some of the striking workers, (or the more active ones) were stripping the fields of all the ripe cocoa pods and selling the wet beans to those small holders who had sweat boxes and drying facilities, and who were willing to buy the stolen produce at discounted prices.

During this time I slept on a mattress in the middle of the dining room floor with the watchman's shotgun and a box of cartridges beside me. I figured that if a man should break in during the night it was necessary to have decided: 1. If I would shoot. 2. Would I fire a warning shot? 3. Would I shoot to kill, or aim for an arm or a leg?

I decided that if someone broke in, they would not be coming to steal; there was plenty of cocoa and nutmegs in the boucan, 100 yards away. This led me to conclude that they could only be coming to kill or maim, so I decided to shoot and aim for the middle of the torso. My intention was not to kill, but with time for one shot only, I had to be sure not to miss. I slept like that for five weeks but I was never put to the test. The rest of the six-week period passed peacefully and we were left unharmed.

Indeed, everything was so peaceful that I would occasionally drive over to Morne Fendue to see my family. On a few occasions I drove into Grenville to buy supplies, and once or twice to St. Georges to attend meetings. On one occasion Denis Henry arranged for a meeting with Administrator Green. We stressed that there had been a complete breakdown of law and order, as the Police were nonfunctional. Mr. Green listened attentively to our protests but offered no promise of greater protection.

It was always with some apprehension that I left Carriere during the strike. There was the fear that there would be an attack on the compound during my absence, or of being stopped by hostile gangs on my journeys. It never happened. I was not shown any hostility during the balance of the episode.

It was with great relief all around that we got the news that the Agricultural Association and the GMMWU had signed an agreement for a wage of five shillings (XCD $1.20) and normal work could resume–with the stipulation that there should be no victimization.

We had nutmeg trees scattered throughout the cocoa fields and a task-worker named Margaret was delegated to visit these trees, collect a basket of nuts, bring them to the boucan, remove the mace, put nuts and mace to dry, and then go home before 11:00 a.m. That was her work for the day. This was a coveted job at a time when many of the workers worked from 7:30 a.m. to 4:00 p.m. This woman had been the main agitator on the first evening. It was Margaret urging the other workers to drag Eldon out and beat him.

On the first day of the resumption of work when I met with Mr. Stanislaus for our usual pre-work conference, I remarked that Margaret had behaved so badly during the strike that we really should remove her from her cushy job but . . . it had been agreed that there should be no victimization–so I thought Mr. Stanislaus understood.

At 7:30 a.m. he left the office to assign the workers to their allotted tasks. I soon heard some grumbling and went out to find that the workers were refusing to resume work unless Margaret was given back her job. Some quick action was required as management must not be seen to give in to workers demands. I called Margaret near and asked her (as if I didn't know), "What are you making all the fuss about?"

"Mr. Stanislaus say I mustn't collect nutmegs," she replied.

"What?! Nutmegs haven't been collected for six weeks! They're rotting on the ground. Go and save as many as you can!"

She took her basket and left and so did the other workers. Thus, was a crisis averted without too much loss of face.

Following the strike the situation between management and workers became very tense. If I approached a gang, they would go silent. I conspired with my cousin, Gordon Gentle, who managed Madeys, a small estate in the parish of St. Patrick's. We believed that the best way to break the ice and restore good relations might be to have a couple of cricket matches between the two estates. It was agreed that the first match should be played at Madeys.

I explained the plan to my workers and they were enthusiastic so I called a meeting of interested players and one said, "But we don't have the money to repair the pitch." There was the semblance of a pitch in the pasture that adjoined the boucan. I said, "I have two hands and two feet. If two fellas will go with me, I will drive the tractor and haul tiff to resurface the pitch if some others will dig up the pitch." They agreed and we repaired the pitch, and cut out the guava bushes that had grown up in the field. We practised assiduously until Madeys' team was ready.

Our team wanted to make me captain, but I protested that I had never been good at cricket but I would play if they wanted me to. Mr. Stanislaus was appointed captain and I was among those selected when he picked our team. We enquired of "old heads" as to what the procedure had been in the old days. We gathered that the visiting team was to be served with, "green tea and salt-fish on biscuit" upon arrival.

The managers were permitted to field two or three of their friends just so long as the teams were balanced. They were expected to contribute XCD $5 each to the kitty. The teams often consisted of 12, 13 or 14 players per side. The visiting team travelled by rented bus, while the managers and friends with families travelled by their cars.

The match started on Sunday at about 10:30 a.m. or whenever all was ready. Madeys won the toss and elected to bat. I retired to the "long on" boundary where I had been sent by our captain, Mr. Stanislaus. He put himself on to bowl and it was not long before he appealed for an LBW (leg before wicket) which was refused. He protested vehemently, other members of the team joined in, and the argument became a quarrel. I approached my captain and asked his permission to leave the field. He was clearly surprised and asked what I meant. I told him, "Mr. Stanislaus, if this is the way you play cricket, it is not the way I play cricket." He said he wanted me to stay so I resumed my fielding position and the game proceeded to a happy conclusion.

All players and spectators repaired to the boucan where we (the visitors) were fed first. The home team was then fed and the wine and rum flowed freely. There were impassioned speeches from both teams. At about 9:00 p.m. the visiting team was helped to our bus and departed for home.

The effect was dramatic. The next day as I approached a gang, someone called out, "Boss! You see that six I hit on that catch I take?" All inhibitions were forgotten and there was harmony once more.

Early the following week we had a meeting of the Carriere players. I told them, "We all work hard all week. On Sunday when we play a match I want to enjoy myself and have fun. I don't want to get involved in arguments and quarrels. As far as I am concerned the umpire's decision is final, but I don't want to spoil your sport. If you want, I will withdraw from the team but continue to assist with the organization." The members asserted that they wanted me to play and agreed to abide by the umpire's decisions.

Some weeks later I addressed the workers before work started. I told them that Madeys had given us a good time and it was our turn to entertain them. The estate gave £10 annually for cricket gear but nothing for entertainment. On payday I would ask Mr. Lazarus (driver) to pass the hat around. I knew that some workers were hard pressed and couldn't give much. I was not asking them to give more than they could afford. If we got a penny, we would give Madeys penny biscuit. If we got two pence, we'd provide penny biscuit and penny salt-fish. On payday to our surprise, Mr. Lazarus took his hat around and collected XCD $58.56 (a large amount at the time). An ex-worker who had become a trafficker even sent a $2 contribution.

On the Saturday before match day I was delegated to go to Grenville to buy salt-beef and fresh beef, salt-pork and fresh pork, cooking oil, flour, biscuits, salt, etc.

Some of the older ladies set up a cookhouse, while space was made in the boucan for tables, benches and chairs. Participants provided table cloths, crockery–often tin plates and cups. We served the visiting team green tea and salt-fish on crackers as we had been instructed by the "old heads." Soon the captains tossed a coin and the game began.

The home-team manager contributed whiskey and during the match it was accepted that if one of the managers hit a six or made a spectacular play, someone would run out with a whiskey and water to reward him. The workers were not permitted this privilege but this did not appear to cause any resentment. Spectators and teams took advantage of available shade and there was much spectator participation. Both at Carriere and at Madeys, the ground sloped considerably so that the shot that earned six runs at one end, produced one or two runs at the other end.

Between innings each team was given a bottle of local rum, either River Antoine or Dumferline. When the match was concluded, all repaired to the boucan where tables and benches had been laid, gas lamps and lanterns hung, and the visitors were fed first. There were neither cutlery, crockery nor benches to accommodate all at one sitting. Those who were not eating, milled around the outside of the building and there was much good-natured banter.

On one occasion, when everyone had eaten and an eloquent worker was making a speech, he frequently proclaimed, "God save the King." My father, who was an honoured guest, corrected him, as Queen Elizabeth II had ascended to the throne. The orator was not deterred and continued to bless the King, while my father continued to correct him, much to the amusement of the assembly. By about 9:00 p.m. all the food and drink had been consumed. The visitors were helped onto their bus and departed. The home team and supporters shut up the buildings and all departed to their homes in excellent good humour.

Those matches became so popular that when I left for St. Lucia there were five estates plus the team from the Cocoa Rehabilitation Scheme participating. Later I was asked to organize a competition. I replied, "When you start a competition, you start a war. I play cricket on Sunday for fun. Leave it so." Peace and harmony continued.

Crochu

Thomson Hankey & Co. was the agent for the new owners of Crochu, and in 1952 they asked me to take over the management of this estate for Major and Mrs. Home-Robertson. The Home-Robertsons were very nice people to work with and I still have the dictionary they sent to me and the silk scarves they sent to Jean and myself.

The property had been previously owned by Sir Joseph De La Mothe, a Belgian, the same condescending man who was the head of the Grenada Agricultural Association. By then he was pretty old and almost blind and almost deaf.

The pay from my employment at Carriere was XCD $144 per month (£30) which was barely adequate to maintain a wife and three children, so I was happy to take on the management of Crochu for an additional $80 per month. That was the reason I accepted the position. When I took over the estate, I thought somebody would come and hand over, but again I just had to go and take over.

The overseer was Mr. Hall and he had absorbed some of De La Mothe's training. We had a patch of grapefruit trees on the estate, I would go down and say, "Mr. Hall I would like 50 grapefruits please." He would call the watchman and send him off to get 50 grapefruits and the fella would come back with a sack over his shoulder and his shirt full of grapefruit. There were precisely 50 grapefruits in the sack, but when he came down from shaking the tree, there were four on the ground. So that's separate!

When Mr. Hall asked me if he could take two pounds of old cocoa to make chocolate, I said, "Sure, Mr. Hall."

"Mr. Lazarus! Mr. Kent say I can have two pound of old cocoa!"

I asked, "What's all that about?"

And he said, "Mr. Kent, you don know? After you gone and dey see me takin' two pound ah cocoa, dey gonna say I t'ief de cocoa!" He was very meticulous.

He gave us a family saying, although I'm probably the only one who remembers it. Trevor used to come down to Crochu during the holidays when he was a schoolboy and when he returned to school on one occasion, Mr. Hall asked, "Mr. Kent, where's Trevor?"

"He had to go back to school," I said.

"Oh," he said, "I like that boy, I really like him. *I like his gait.*"

The buildings on the estate were in dreadful condition. The

overseer's kitchen had a 2' hole in the middle of the floor. I don't know for how many years they had been manoeuvring around this, and I only wrote to tell the owners about this house in particular, and the other buildings. And they wrote to me and Hankeys immediately, agreeing to the rebuilding of all the estate buildings. We rebuilt the overseer's house.

There were three or four houses on the estate where workers had been given permission to build their houses. People had been living there for twenty or thirty years but the estate was sold "free of all encumbrances," and although it was the responsibility of the De La Mothe family to move them, they did not. I went and spoke to these people and I was able to get two of the three families living on the estate to move by giving them assistance to move their house, and in one case finding a spot for them and paying for it. My philosophy was, anything but litigation. The lady in the one remaining house felt that Sir Joseph owed her something because the road down to the works at Crochu was so bad that Sir Joseph never went down there. He would pay at this lady's house near the public road. I was getting along all right with her until a fly-by-night lawyer came along and started advising her, and it was about this time I was preparing to go to St. Lucia. I told Hankeys that I was not prepared to come back from St. Lucia; I had done what I could and handed it over to them as the agent. So that house is probably still there, I don't know.

Crochu was very low on the list of estates in Grenada, maybe thirtieth or thereabouts–small in size and reputation–a poor cousin. We only had about twenty-five workers on the estate, but in no time it had the best overseer's house on the island.

The planters in Grenada found themselves in a difficult position because after the Second World War, the price of "fine estate cocoa" had shot up to £2,000/ton (XCD $9,600) on the world market while the cocoa producers received 4s 2p (XCD $1) per pound for fine estate cocoa. In no time at all the price of fine estate cocoa had fallen, and the cocoa producers were getting 2s 1p (50 cents) so if, when the price went up, they adjusted the workers' wages accordingly, when the price dropped they would not be able to reduce the wages. So when Christmastime came along I wrote to the owners and said I thought it would be more fair to give the workers a bonus when we had a good year. The Home-Robertsons cabled me back immediately, authorizing a bonus of 30 shillings for the men, and 25s for the women. It was not a substantial amount but I'm pretty sure this was the first bonus ever paid in Grenada. Men were working for about 5s per day (XCD $1), so it was equivalent to about a week's pay, which was not bad. It was amazing how that bonus bought their loyalty. This was after the Gairy strike in '51 and although Gairy called another strike about three years later, it was not successful and went to arbitration.

It was about an eight-mile drive from Carriere to Crochu and I went there about twice a week. The workers came to me to say they had no grievance, and asked if they should strike. Again, I was faced with a dilemma, I didn't want their houses to burn down, so I told them to go home and lay low. Then the matter went to arbitration, and it's the only case I ever heard of where the arbitrator gave nothing. But that's another story. . . .

I managed Crochu for about six years, and I took it from 78 bags of cocoa per annum to 135, almost double by the time I left. This small estate also produced 3 tons of copra per annum, and our last crop was 17 tons per annum. I found the carcass of an old canal which was no longer running and took my cutlass and walked up it for a quarter of a mile to where it originally started at a small stream and found there was a dam broken. I had the canal cleaned out, got a mason and we repaired the dam without any big flourish. We diverted the water into the coconut field with a series of contour drains. That explains this jump in copra production.

Hurricane
Janet

Jean and I went to Barbados in September of 1955 when I was delegated by the Grenada Agriculturists' Union to represent them at an Employers' Federation meeting. Whilst there we heard of the approaching Hurricane Janet, which in early stages was believed to be tracking north of Barbados. Then it swerved, and during the night we were awakened by the Rediffusion (a system for distributing radio or TV programs) coming on at around midnight.

The governor announced that the storm was heading straight for Barbados! Then a bit later he came on again to say that the storm was passing a bit south of Barbados and that we should pray in turn for the people of St. Lucia and then St. Vincent. Then there was a complete news blackout.

All night the wind howled and there was light rain. Although I couldn't say what the speed of the wind was, we were all hunkered down until dawn. I wanted to go out and see the condition of the sea but sheets of galvanized were still flying and I was persuaded to remain indoors. As soon as it was safe to go out, I went to the beach to observe the sea in Carlisle Bay. I could see several trees were down, roofs had gone and galvanized fences were strewn around. The sea was tremendous, breaking far out, and as soon as the waves crested, the wind blew the tops off. Of the five boats at anchor the evening before, only one remained. As I watched, a big wave broke over it and it sank.

Although we went to the office of Cable and Wireless there was a complete news blackout regarding Grenada and they could tell us nothing. Later we heard that a small plane en route to Barbados had flown over and described Grenada as devastated. The airport at Pearls was strewn with big boulders and big trees, a virtual river flowed down the airstrip to the sea. No aircraft would be able to land there for many weeks.

We had left our four children with various friends. Diana was on Green Island, and the two younger boys (Peter and William) were at my father's home at Morne Fendue which was a very strong building. Trevor was with my brother-in-law at Marli which was an old wooden house, and we feared for it and for him.

On the evening following the passage of Hurricane Janet on Barbados we searched for and found a freighter leaving that evening bound for Grenada via St. Vincent, and we were able to get deck-passage on it. We were in St. Vincent next morning and as we came down the chain of islands, although Bequia was green, they got progressively darker, from a light khaki colour to black; Grenada was black. As we approached Grenada, the sea was discoloured and strewn with trees, branches, bush, coconuts, breadfruits, cocoa pods, etc. There was nothing green. Grenada was just black with red scars streaming down the hillsides where gigantic mud slides had gouged the hillsides exposing the red mud below. It was not until we got down to St. George's outer harbour and anchored that we saw the first vestige of green down toward Point Saline in the southwest. We could see that several buildings were damaged and as we entered the harbour, we saw that the pier was gone. My brother-in-law Keith Mancini (who was Huggins' shipping agent) came onboard and we learned from him that our children were safe, but the Grand Ètang route was blocked, the east coast road was blocked, the west coast road was blocked. With his help, we got passage on the *M.V. Daerwood,* a small freighter that plied to Trinidad. We learned that she was leaving St. George's at 4:30 a.m. to go around to Gouyave, Victoria, Sauteurs and eventually on to Grenville, dropping bags of rice, flour and other supplies. Our home at Carriere was about four miles from Grenville and Morne Fendue was another 4 miles further on.

We embarked on the *Daerwood* and as we travelled up the coast around to Grenville, we could better see the damage. We disembarked in Grenville and we got a lift to Pearls Airport but had to walk from there, since both Dumferline and Pearls bridges had been washed away. As we walked, we could see the trees, large rocks and mud covering the airstrip, and the damage to houses and cultivation. Cocoa and nutmeg trees were broken or uprooted, and on all sides people were hammering away, trying to provide shelter for their families.

We got to Carriere midmorning to find that the house was unharmed, the boucan and drying rooms were unharmed, the flimsy office building of rotting boards and shingles which sat on top of the windmill tower was unharmed. Quite amazing. My Morris Oxford car also appeared to be unharmed, and the overseer told us that a big hog plum tree about 15" in diameter had fallen over the car, but it was saved by a 3" concrete wall adjacent to the garage that the tree was resting on, suspended over the car.

By this time there were gangs clearing the road and we were able to drive over to Morne Fendue. Everyone figured Morne Fendue would be undamaged. The walls of the house itself were constructed of heavy stone, two feet thick, and upstairs eighteen inches thick. The wind had blown in a whole casement window in "Mother's Room" and although the 1/4" thick plate glass was undamaged, the wind had taken the roof off "Daddy's Room." We gathered the two younger children and went back to Carriere. Our ten-year-old daughter Diana had survived the hurricane in the care of the DeGale family on Green Island, located off the northeast coast of Grenada which was accessed by row boat. Fortunately the caretaker had pulled the boat high up the beach, so it was not swept away, but they had to wait until the afternoon to cross back to the mainland. Diana then had to walk about three miles, climbing over fallen trees and debris to get to Montrose, the DeGale family home. From there she walked to Morne Fendue and then down to Trevellan, which was another family home that was also left undamaged. Trevor was at Marli, and nothing happened to Marli which is inland above Grenville on the way up to Grand Ètang.

We resumed life at Carriere where the estate buildings were undamaged but the cultivation was in a shambles. Cocoa trees, nutmeg trees, and in a few cases, coconut trees, were down on all sides. Where previously one could see only about fifty feet in any direction, now one could see four, five or six hundred yards in many directions. The workers resumed work, cutting down or propping up cocoa trees and cutting out those that were too badly damaged to revive.

As president of the GAU I had to make my way to St. George's as soon as I could, to pick up the reins. It was some two weeks before I got to Carriacou and was able to see for myself the devastation that had been caused. Nearly every building on Carriacou was damaged in one way or another. A number of lives were lost. I knew of one lady who left the Bogles crossroads to walk to her home along the coast and was never seen or heard of again. It was believed that she was blown out to sea. Several vessels were washed ashore but many took refuge in the harbour or the oyster beds at Windward, and survived. The Anglican church lost its roof and the Catholic church was damaged too. Many small houses either lost their roofs or were blown away. Even the stone structures like Belvedere House and the Anglican rectory had their second stories so badly damaged that they were cut down and made into bungalows. As for Craigston House, the whole structure was blown away, leaving just the stone walls that surround the cellar. A good part of the factory roof that covered the still was also blown away.

It is reputed that during a hurricane in the northern hemisphere, the northern section of the hurricane gets higher winds, and the higher rainfall is in the southern section. That may be why Carriacou got more wind damage and Grenada got more rain damage. Wind speeds at Pearls reached 135 mph before the instrument blew away, and one can only guess at what speed was reached on Carriacou. It was reported that the sign that read PEARLS AIRPORT was found on Carriacou. I can't say whether it got there by air or by sea.

As many householders depended upon drums kept near their houses for water, and as many of these had either been blown away or overturned, water was at a premium. It was then that the big steel tank was erected in Hillsborough between Main Street and the sea. In the interim, water was obtained from the big cisterns at Dumfries, The Anglican Rectory, Craigston, and Top Hill.

Meanwhile, back in Grenada, the GAU got in touch with the Employers' Federation and the Chamber of Commerce and we agreed to host a meeting at the Empire Cinema on the Thursday following Hurricane Janet. I found myself chairing the meeting. After much discussion from the members it was agreed that an appeal for help for the agricultural sector should be written to the governor, and that it should be written by the Agriculturists' Union. This fell into my lap. I shut myself into my office at Carriere for 24 hours and wrote the appeal. This appeal was presented at a similar joint meeting in St. George's on the following Thursday, and was unanimously accepted. Sir Denis Henry added one clause asking that it be free of political interference.

A delegation of four members took the appeal to Governor Colville Deverell and presented it to him and he undertook to forward it to Colonial Office. Some three weeks later Governor Deverell sent for me and told me that Colonial Office had lent XCD $16 million; $11.5 million was to go to the Government of Grenada and $4.5 million was to be administered by a nebulous organization called the Central Agricultural Rehabilitation Committee (CARC). He asked me to nominate ten area chairmen to process applications for loans to farmers in the country. These sub committees were dotted around the island to make it easy for farmers to apply for assistance. The CARC comprised these ten members plus the attorney general, Mr. Keith Alleyne, the director of agricultural rehabilitation, Mr. Tubby Wright, the superintendent of agriculture, Mr. Will Nanton and Mr. John Mordecai, who was a permanent secretary in the government of Jamaica and on leave in England when he volunteered to come and assist us. He was really the head of the CARC.

We advertised for applications for assistance. We had been told that in Dominica in previous years such funds for hurricane damage from the UK had been given to planters in large sums and in many cases the money did not get used for agricultural rehabilitation. One planter opened a bay rum factory, another opened a supermarket and one opened a cinema. So we were resolved not to give the money out in lump sums, but to disperse it in installments.

The money was loaned on very generous terms; twenty years interest-free, another five years at 3.5%. The farmers would apply for a sum and the area committees would meet to approve the applications. The area committees consisted of two representatives from large plantations, two peasant farmers, the agricultural officer and the roads' officer. It was figured that these six people would know the applicants in their area and the extent of their property. A fellow might apply and say he had ten acres of nutmegs that were completely destroyed and the committee would say, ". . . but the man only has three acres of land." It was the responsibility of the committee to sort out what was a legitimate request and recommend the approval of a loan. Most of the larger plantations could do a week's or a month's work and then apply for an installment to be dispersed.

My committee met in my office every Monday for months. We sometimes met up until eight o'clock at night, at which stage we would have to move up to my home because there was no electricity in my office. Every Thursday the chair of these ten committees met with the CARC. We would go through the applications that were recommended from the subcommittee and decide, then John Mordecai and his secretary would do the donkey work, preparing and signing cheques.

We were going along happily until we discovered that Colonial Office had stipulated that money should only be lent out on first mortgage. Then we found out that nearly every square metre of land on Grenada was mortgaged. We were stymied.

At the next meeting of CARC, John Mordecai said to me before the meeting started, "Ed, I want you to move that CARC will lend money on second mortgage."

I protested, "But John, we can't do it."

And he said, "Don't worry man, you just do as I ask you."

So I moved the motion and got Willie Branch to second it, and it was passed unanimously. That afternoon John Mordecai went to the governor and said, "Sir, I've come to inform you of something the CARC did today. I can't ask your permission, because I know it is irregular, but we have agreed to lend money on second mortgages."

Governor Deverell said, "You can't do that."

And John Mordecai said, "But sir, we've done it."

Governor Deverell said, "Well, we'll have to notify Colonial Office by cable," and John said, "Yes sir, that's why I've come to you."

Then Deverell said, "Well, you worked in Colonial Office, you know how they think, so you write the cable and I'll sign it."

This was done. About a month later, after we had already lent out $1.5 million the approval came from Colonial Office.

It had been stressed to us by John Mordecai that in his experience dealing with hurricanes in Jamaica, it was very important to get people moving immediately following the disaster as people soon got accustomed to seeing trees down, utility poles down, bridges gone, etc., and people got complacent. So it was necessary to act urgently, and we had.

There was another hurdle to overcome. We found that in many cases the occupier of land was not the sole owner. There might have been five or six siblings and some of them had gone abroad and the one who remained in Grenada thought that the land was theirs because they were paying the taxes. We realised that if we went lending money to these partial owners and the others came back and claimed the land, although we had a second mortgage it was worthless. The other owners had not signed or received any of this mortgage money. People were mortgaging land they had no authority to.

With the aid of the attorney general and the legal department, a law was drafted which provided that in a case like this, notices would be posted around the farm for a period of a month, stating that it was the intention of the CARC to lend the owner money on this particular lot of land, and if anybody had any knowledge as to the whereabouts of the other owners, would they please come forward. If at the end of that time nobody had come forward, we would lend the money.

A fund was set up to cover this contingency and a small percentage of all the loans was put into this fund. The property was valued so that if someone came back in ten years time they would be compensated for their share of the value from that fund. I never heard of it being used before I went away, and the CARC continued to function well. You saw work going on all over the island where people were cleaning up their lands. We had inspectors who would ensure work had been completed before approving further disbursements.

During the next year (1956) tremendous strides were made in the rehabilitation of the cocoa and nutmeg fields. In 1953 I had taken my holiday and got deck passage on a banana boat to Dominica, where I spent two weeks learning as much as I could about bananas. Fortunately, at Carriere I had planted bananas, which is an ideal nurse crop for the rehabilitation of cocoa and nutmeg fields, and an excellent short-term crop because within a year you can be harvesting bananas, whereas with cocoa you might have to wait three years, and with nutmeg you might have to wait five or six years.

In 1955 the GAU was very strong and the government referred to them on many cases, as to strategy and timing of different projects. They sought input and expertise from the GAU. Within a few years of my going away to St. Lucia the GAU more or less dwindled. Denis Henry went to live in England, and I don't think anybody really took it over. The difference between the rehabilitation of agriculture following Hurricane Janet and Hurricane Ivan in 2004, was like chalk and cheese. Following Hurricane Ivan, there was nothing like the GAU or CARC. I heard of no loans to farmers, and government had an extraordinary scheme of sending work gangs onto people's property to cut and clean, and they would pay them, but they didn't give money directly to landowners. From what I heard it didn't work very well. You can imagine, when a fellow is working for himself and it's his money he's spending he takes responsibility.

Springs Estate

Springs Estate belonged to a dear lady in her nineties, a Mrs. Kernahan. My brother-in-law Keith Mancini, who had been the manager, got involved in another venture and asked me if I would take it on. And I did, for an additional XCD $80 per month, which was still the standard going rate. So now I was managing three estates simultaneously.

Springs was a relatively small estate, 150 acres up in the middle belt of Grenada. It was mostly nutmeg. The extent of the devastation of Hurricane Janet can be indicated by the fact that the year before the hurricane, Springs produced 100,000 lbs. of green nutmeg, and the year following Janet, it produced 8,000 lbs. The beginning of the estate's fiscal year was September 1st, so most of that 8,000 lbs. was collected between the first and the twenty-third day of September. Practically nothing.

Keith told me I would have to go on board the Viscount plane at Pearls to meet Mrs. Kernahan and "hand her off." So I was ready, I let the other passengers come down and I went aboard and greeted her. She had a white gentleman travelling with her but she hung onto my arm and I handed her down the steps. We were going into the terminal building, and halfway to the door she turned around and said, "Mac! Do you have my papers?"

And he said, "Yes Bella. Don't worry about it. I have everything."

"Mac! I didn't ask you that. Do you have my papers?"

This fella she was talking to was Charles McEnearney, the founder of McEnearney Motors, a very big Trinidadian company established in 1919, Trinidad's first Ford dealership.

I got them into a taxi and taken to their hotel in St. George's and arranged that she would come up to the estate the following day.

I had to borrow a Land Rover from my friend to show her around. Nearly all the planters were claiming ruination and poverty, and as I drove her around (very gingerly) she said, "Oh things are not too bad, Mr. Kent. Look! I see a nutmeg tree. Look there! I see two cocoa trees," when perhaps there was one tree in a hollow here and there.

I explained my plan to her of planting bananas as a short-term crop with quick return and she said, "Don't you think we should do something about Baptiste's salary?" Baptiste was the overseer. I thought, Lord, here's another one.

I said, "Well, you know Mrs. Kernahan, nutmegs were easy. Now Mr. Baptiste is going to have to work much harder."

"Well, that's what I mean! Don't you think we should raise his salary?"

Amazing! I hastily agreed.

Springs had beautiful soil and in no time at all it was producing eight and ten-hand bunches of bananas. The estate was situated on a hill with a road along the crest that led to the buildings, with a river on each side of the hill. The bananas were growing in the valleys and on the hillsides.

On a subsequent occasion (when she had another "Mac" along as her bagman) I said, "You know Mrs. Kernahan, I really feel sorry for these poor women. To haul these bananas up this hill, it's really hard on them."

"Oh!" she said, "Mr. Kent, I quite agree with you. Why don't we cut some roads?"

So I said, "Mrs. Kernahan, there are only two bulldozers on the island; one belongs to Government and one belongs to Mr. Branch at Dougaldston, and neither of them are for rent."

"Oh," she said, "Nonsense! Why don't the planters put together and buy one?"

I said, "The trouble is that the planters with money have no ideas, and the planters with ideas have no money."

"Oh," she said, "Nonsense. Mac! When you get back to Trinidad, you buy a tractor for me and send it to Mr. Kent."

Of course she was a big shareholder in McEnearney`s and they were the Ford agent and they sold tractors. Then she told me, "Now Mr. Kent, this is not for Springs Estate. This is just between you and me. I will provide the tractor, you will run it, and we will split the profit."

To my surprise the tractor came. We cut roads and we rented it out. We rented it to Springs Estate and I kept meticulous accounts. It was difficult to find someone who knew how to drive it, so whenever the driver was ill or attending a christening or something, I would get on it and I learned how to drive it. This was fortuitous and stood me in good stead up at Dennery later on when a recalcitrant driver was being fractious and he told me, "I could go home, you know! I could go home now!"

I said, "Do just that." I took the keys from him and he was amazed to see me get on the tractor and drive it.

Mrs. Kernahan really was a lovely lady. Her husband had left her a big coconut estate down in the south of Trinidad at Cedros. She told me how in 1920 she was in England when she got a telegram to say that 90% of the coconuts were down. She said, "I started packing, then I said, 'Bella! You're a fool. You'll probably never be able to afford a holiday in England again. You can't push back up the trees. You might just as well stay here and enjoy your holiday.' She was a very practical person.

I persuaded her to make use of the soft loan from CARC although she didn't want to get into debt, and then the money from bananas kept coming in, and in no time at all I had XCD $30,000 on fixed deposit with Barclay's, and here we were borrowing money! And all from bananas!

Before the hurricane, Grenada exported 30,000 bags of dried polished cocoa. I hate to quote figures but I think it had got back to around 20,000 (although that sounds too good to be true, but it recovered a lot). We replanted some of the cocoa, then we replanted some of the nutmegs. We were on the road to recovery when this offer came from St. Lucia which was too good for me to turn down.

Dennery
Factory Co. Ltd.

Denis Barnard's family owned Dennery Factory Co. Ltd. When I came to Dennery, no one came to hand over to me, I just had to take over. This happened several times during my career.

There was no middle management. There were ten overseers and a stockman called Mr. Charlie who looked after the herd of 140 cattle. Mr. Charlie rode a horse, which gave him some elevation (in more ways than one) and he was much feared by the workers because he would tell Denis all that was going on in the valley. It was a big valley, two and a half thousand acres, and several villages.

Every Thursday afternoon Denis went to Castries, so every Wednesday, while Denis lounged on his big couch, Charlie would come up the front steps and sit, not on the verandah level, but one step down–he knew his place–and he would tell Denis who was *t'iefing*, who was not working, who was sleeping with whom . . . everything. So Charlie was feared for his knowledge, and his access to Mr. Barnard.

On one particular Monday morning when I went up to Dennery from my home in Castries, Charlie told me that the cattle broke out of the corral and damaged a man's garden. The man wanted compensation, but Charlie told him to *hush he mouth* because his house was on company land, and *in the company he makin' a bread.* So I told Charlie, "I'm not happy with that," and asked him to send Mr. Joseph to see me.

Now I had started calling people *Mr. Joseph,* and *Mr. Charlie,* something that was unheard of. A little boy would come to me and say, "Benny say... so and so," or "Benny say... this or that," and I would say, "Who? Oh, you mean *Mr. Benny*! Ah, now I understand."

I was sitting in this broken down office (the floor was broken and the place was in very poor condition, like the Scottish expression, where there's muck there's brass) when the hackles on my neck went up. I looked around and there was a man standing there with a face like thunder! So I said, "Are you Mr. Joseph?"

"Yeah."

"Come Mr. Joseph, come." I said. "Now let's get this straight. When your cow damage the company bananas, we does make you pay. When the company cow damage your bananas, we will pay."

Blank face.

"So, you got that?"

Blank face, no response.

"So, all that is in dispute is the quantum. Man, do you really think you can get $5 for a stool of corn? When you consider you wife have to break the corn, and dry it, and she have to get on a bus and go in Castries to sell the corn, do you really think you could get $5?"

Blank. Absolute dead blank.

So I said, "Well alright, let's leave that aside. What about the ground nuts? You want $3 for a stool, man. $3 for groundnuts? How much do you think you can get a pound? Groundnuts selling for .60 cents a pound and you want three dollars!"

Blank.

"Well, let's try the pigeon peas." I heard a noise and I looked up and he was going out the door. I said, "Where you going, man? I don't want you to leave before we make bargain."

The man stood in the doorway and he told me, "It's all right, since you tell me the company cow damage me garden and the company pay, it's all right, I don't want no money at all," and he walked away.

I think his pride was hurt when Charlie told him he should *hush he mouth.* But when I told him he had rights as a man and the company would pay, that was enough. He accepted the fact that he was a man who had rights. I don't know whether he just made up the figure thinking he wouldn't get paid (he was hoping) but he knew before Edward Kent, he would not have been paid. Think of the rancour, the hatred that would have festered in that man's heart over this injustice, for the rest of his life, and for what? It didn't cost the company anything, except ten minutes of my time.

The flat lands of the valley were all planted in cane for the production of sugar and, its by-product, rum. There were nine miles of rail line, this was before the days of easy trucking. One of my jobs was to take up most of this rail line and make roads where most of this rail line was laid. We had a stone quarry, and a tiff quarry, which somehow fell under the aegis of the general manager. Apart from the ten overseers on the agricultural side, there was a quarry gang and a tiff quarry gang, and carpenters and masons, and the transport division; we had five trucks for hauling bananas, fertiliser, rum etc. All the rail lines were taken up and stacked, we couldn't leave them lying around the place, and people did buy them for reinforcement for their homes, so that was another job I had–to sell rail line at so much per foot.

The hierarchy starting at the top was Denis Barnard, who did not participate in the management of the estate, but took full responsibility for the distillery. Under him was the general manager (myself). Next, was Mr. Montrose, who was the paymaster, and Mr. O'Geest who was the secretary, he wrote letters, kept accounts, etc. Lower down the line was Mr. Goddard, who was in full control of funds distribution, accounts payable and the payroll. Lance DeLisle, was the engineer (he was Frank DeLisle's brother, the fella who started LIAT). He had lived in my house on the estate, but he had been given notice to leave after I arrived in November. The cane crop was coming up, and by June he was to go, so Denis asked him to move into a house for an overseer in the valley with the cane. I felt bad about having had him turfed out, but he was only there until June.

Mr. Charlie was a law unto himself, generally down in Fond D'or (on his horse) at the bottom of the valley. He took the cattle out to graze every day and penned them up every night (that became one of my jobs too–to see that the cattle were regularly sprayed, because the area down there teemed with ticks) That is partly where I got my experience with cattle, but we didn't know anything about butchering or selling, we kept the cattle to make a dollar. Denis didn't lose an opportunity to make a dollar. He even kept chickens down at the factory. Because he was paying 40% income tax, he would take these eggs to his friends in Castries every Thursday, where he got cash in hand, free of tax.

There's a lovely story attached to that. The British government sent a man and his wife out to assist the St. Lucian government in plugging holes in the income tax legislation. Our accountant, Willie Rapier, told Denis that this man was querying the fact that he saw records for a lot of poultry feed but he didn't see any sales. Denis told Willie, "Send the man up, tell him to come up Wednesday afternoon."

So the fella came up and I was there when Denis said, "Look man, you're complaining about no sales of poultry. This was a typographical error by Willie's office. It was not poultry feed, it was dog food. Look here, where Ed and I live on this complex, we could have watchmen with guns patrolling around the perimeter fence all around the compound all night, every night. This would cost a fortune, so instead of that we keep dogs. And these dogs eat a lot of food!"

At around 5:00 p.m. Denis called for drinks and the whiskey started to flow. I sat dutifully. Because the factory flooded when there was heavy rain, we had this area where the big generators were located that supplied electricity for the factory and for us and a few chosen others. We had a system where the lights used to blink at half-past nine and then the lights went out at ten. So at half-past nine, with no thought of dinner–we were down to serious business and this English fellow was picking holes in some other accounts which Denis was rebutting–the lights blinked. Denis asked me to call down to the factory, but I didn't get the watchman so I went down and asked him to keep the generator on until half-past ten. Would you believe that at half-past ten the lights blinked and I went down and asked him to keep it on until eleven, and then I went straight home. I believe those people stayed there 'till about two o'clock. Absolute strangers to the island, they didn't know their way around and they had to drive sixteen miles into Castries, then another eight miles to their hotel.

Every morning at about 6:45 a.m. Mr. Charlie would have a horse sent up to my home and by seven o'clock I was down at the factory to be faced by carpenters, masons, road gang, rail line gang, quarry gang and the transport division, all waiting for instructions. I had bought myself a car when I first arrived and I used this to drive to Dennery but I would ask Mr. Charlie to have a horse waiting for me at a certain spot. I would drive up there and by the time the horse was coming up, I had already inspected a few sections, then I would get on the horse and ride into the hinterland. They had some cocoa up there and I was very keen, having been a "cocoa man" in Grenada. The cocoa was covered down in vines and we were hacking our way through it when I suddenly thought about poisonous snakes and I jumped and said to the overseer, "Gregor, you don't have these fer-de-lance up here, the deadly ones? You only have the tete chein, the serpent that has a head like a dog?"

He said, "Yes sir."

I asked, "But they're harmless, aren't they?"

He said, "Yes sir, but if they bite you, you dead."

I got out of there at high speed, I tell you.

The overseers were all reasonable fellows, and Denis told me that when I first came people liked me, but now they disliked me because they couldn't "time me." Everywhere they turned, I was there. In the afternoon when I had nothing to do, I would go roaming around some of the fields. I was admonished by Mr. Benny because about three years before, the manager of an adjoining estate had suspected his coconuts were being stolen. On one Sunday after lunch he went out and surprised the people stealing coconuts, he started to run but they chopped him up. Not seeing his father, the man's son went looking for him, but the t'iefs spied him before he spied them, and he started to run. He tripped and fell into a drain and they chopped him up too. Two men hanged for that crime so you can imagine Mr. Benny's concern. But I was accustomed to roaming around the fields in Grenada and Mr. Benny would say, "Mr. Kent, you mustn't do that you know! Supposing you meet somebody!" *Well, supposing I do?* I thought, but it never really sank in that I could be chopped up. My moves were unpredictable because I believed that if you didn't show the flag, things started to go down. The best manure for any land is the tramp of the manager's foot.

Denis had given six months warning that he was closing down the sugar factory, because everybody brought cane to Dennery (the way everybody brought limes to Craigston). He was closing it down because it was uneconomic. Two years before I left, he had spent £45,000 modernizing the factory. But with the cost of labour and the price of sugar low, although he ran a fairly tight outfit, he couldn't make money. He had planted 200 acres of bananas and the return from that outperformed the sugar by far, so that's when he decided to close it down.

During my very first year as soon as the cane was harvested, my job was to go in with the TD18 tractor and plow the cane fields and plant bananas. We only had one tractor and sometimes we didn't even wait on the tractor, but what I know is that during that first year we planted 317 acres of bananas. When I say we, I mean the overseers and workers who were not too busy harvesting cane, but as soon as they were finished harvesting, we had to get cracking. Pretty soon, Dennery was by far the biggest banana-producer in the Eastern Caribbean. I had a compliment paid to me by the Geest manager, an Englishman, who said, "I used to say that Dennery fruit was about the worst in the island, but now it is about the best." You think Denis liked that? Denis didn't like that, at all. However, I weathered that.

Mr. Palmer was a peasant farmer and he had 30 acres of flat land and he produced 300 tons of cane per year. What I liked about him was that when you passed a field you couldn't tell who was the boss, he was working like everybody else. He produced 300-tons of cane at XCD $10 per ton, his gross for the year was XCD $3,000 and he had to pay his workers, etc. I was on my horse in those days, and one day I passed by and saw him sitting disconsolately on a culvert. I said, "Mr. Palmer, why don't you plant bananas, man?" And he said, "Mr. Kent, I don't know nothing about bananas. All me life it's cane I growing."

I said, "It's not difficult, if I can give you some help, I'd be glad to, but it's not difficult. Try, try."

He got up off his fanny and went and planted bananas and in eighteen months he was shipping about $1,500 worth of bananas every fortnight. Nearly $40,000/year. One day I met him in the road and said, "Mr. Palmer, what do you think about the bananas now?"

"Mr. Kent, to tell you the truth it is only now I beginning to understand the value of the estate my father left to me," he said. He built a good-sized concrete house up on stilts–everybody was up on stilts in this valley because of flooding–and I kept seeing him sit on that culvert just gazing at his house. He couldn't believe it was his and he just sat on that culvert admiring it.

Although the whole valley was about two and a half thousand acres, Denis would say, "Ed man, I feel constrained, confined by these hills. We should expand."

It had been well understood when I went to St. Lucia that Dennery would absorb all of my time. Not like in Grenada where I managed two other estates and was president of the Agriculturists' Association. Sometimes when having our drinks, Denis would say, "Ed, you know Balenbouche, that's a fine estate." Balenbouche Estate was situated on the south coast, opposite the Soufriere in St. Vincent and when it erupted in 1902, a lot of ash settled there. Balenbouche got almost a metre of ash and they had rivers on both sides. "We could use that water you know. There's nobody between us and the sea, so we can take it all, and they have beautiful soil."

And I would agree and say, "Yes Denis, but who is going to manage it?" and all our castles would come tumbling down.

At Denis' behest, we took in some hillsides where the land was not so good, but I think he just wanted to increase production. If we were producing 10,000 bunches per week, he wanted to produce 12,000 bunches per week. I granted his wish, but it took a lot of work. Particularly because I took on the responsibility for all the shipping, and there were about a hundred sheds, spread out over 1,300 acres of land. By the time I left I had three assistant managers, it was necessary to delegate. I had one assistant manager named Mr. Cassah from Trinidad, one named Moncherie from St. Lucia, and Denis' son Laurie. They would bring in reports from all the different sheds, by midmorning they would give Denis the latest figures (so I would have an idea if the cut was going up or down). I wanted to know as soon as possible what the production from each field was, for each week. If a field produced 100 bunches last week, and it produced 87 bunches this week, well, *one swallow does not a summer make,* (I wanted an idea if the cut was going up or down) and I kept a running account. The next report would come in and now perhaps it was 93 and then it was 82, and the next one would come in and it was 74 and now it's only 62, and I get the impression the cut is going down. But if it's the other way around, then I get the impression that it's going up throughout the valley and I have to be on my kee-vee to provide trucks. We had as many as seventeen trucks, apart from five of our own. When I went down in the morning, there would be seventeen trucks streamed off down the road. My first Christmas at Dennery I got baskets of gifts–yams, dasheen, plantain, sweet potato, even some poultry!–from the truckers. But I said, "Thank you very much but it won't make any difference. First come, first served." I had a man named Mr. French in charge of dispatching all the hired trucks and we paid him a small commission. He organized the trucks and provided a list at the end of the cutting, and we paid him–and he paid them. So it worked very well.

Tuesday, Wednesday and Thursday of every week was absorbed by shipping bananas. The most we ever shipped were 14,400 bunches in one week. The banana boat arrived at Vieux Fort, St. Lucia on a Tuesday, then came around to Castries on Wednesday and Thursday, but with that volume of fruit we wanted to get some out earlier, we couldn't ship it all in two days. As general manager I had to find a way, so on Tuesday we would ship on a limited cut (not everybody cut, I would tell who was to cut for Tuesday, just enough to fill our trucks, not the hired trucks) to the boat before it reached Castries. We sold to Geest through the Banana Association and they paid us so much per ton for freight to go to Castries, but we would be shipping a little further to Vieux Fort. It was worth it for us to be able to get rid of a third of our fruit on Tuesday as it was less stressful Wednesday and Thursday. The station would stay open all night and close at eight o'clock in the morning. I would be out on the road–there was one central place where a lot of fruit still came out on wagons before we laid in all the roads–fruit would be coming in and I would be checking to see if shed 83 is clear, or is shed 26 clear, and sending people off to check and then when I saw the amount of fruit we had left I could gauge our trucking requirements. We would send our own trucks out first and sometimes they made two or three trips in a day. If they left four hours ago, one hour to get there . . . I would have to wait, (I would be out until late, mosquitos chewing me up) then if I didn't see the trucks coming back, I would drive 3/4 mile to my home to ring Castries (telephone operator, you know) to ask them to put me through to the weigh bridge. At the weigh bridge I would ask them if they could tell me about Dennery trucks; are there any around? And they would say, "One just leave," and I would have to figure out . . . if we've got three truckloads of bananas and one just left . . . I'd dash to Dennery town, which was about three miles away and try to rustle up a truck. If our cut was going up, probably the peasant farmers' cut was going up too, and they also hired these trucks, so I had to get in early.

I did have a compliment paid to me by Denis when I was away for three months and Laurie was left in charge for the first time. The contract Denis gave me included three months leave, every three years, with first class passage paid to England for my wife and myself. And when I came back, Denis told me, "I told Laurie for the first time in the history of Dennery that fruit had been left back in sheds." But he also said to me once, "The trouble with you is that you want to do everything yourself."

And I said, "Denis, you just give me some competent staff and you'll see how quickly I leave it to them." As Truman said, the buck stops here.

It was a great experience and I learned a lot. When I went to St. Lucia in 1957, I was a babe in arms, and when I left in 1968 I was a fairly mature man.

Duke of Edinburgh's
Commonwealth Study
Conference '62

Duke of Edinburgh's
Commonwealth Study Conference

At Dennery the truck would bring up mail from Castries on Wednesdays and on one such Wednesday when I received some mail (which was unusual) there was an imposing looking envelope which was stamped on the back with a Latin inscription; *honi soit qui mal y pense* (evil to him who evil thinks). When I opened it, to my amazement I saw the letterhead was from Buckingham Palace. It was written in ink and began, "Dear Mr. Kent," and I looked at the end and it was signed, "Philip."

Prince Philip was inviting me to attend the second Commonwealth Study Conference, which he had started six years earlier. The first one was in Oxford. At Prince Philip's insistence the conference members were to be "people who appeared likely to be in the next generation of leaders, so that when the time came for them to make important decisions they would have the benefit of what they had discovered on the Study Conference to help them." He made it plain that if I attended, I would be attending as an individual not as a delegate representing my country, or my island, or my company; I would just be representing myself. A personal invitation. He went on to say that in following The Queen around, he noted that the Commonwealth was making the same mistakes as Britain had made in industrialisation. In England, coal had been discovered, coal mines had sprung up, people had come in to work from the surrounding villages and there was no planning for schools or other infrastructure, like water, sewage, etc. So he had invited three hundred people from all over the Commonwealth six years before, to discuss these problems, and to discuss whether the Commonwealth might be spared from making the same mistakes. That was the gist of it.

The Conference would start in Montreal, Quebec in April of 1962 and end in Vancouver, British Columbia in May. Well of course I jumped at the opportunity but I had to twist Denis' arm a bit to give me the time off.

When this Conference was a germ of an idea, Prince Philip parked the Royal Yacht *Britannia* in the St. Lawrence Seaway. He held a dinner to which he invited the CEOs of Shell, Seagram's, Anglo-Canadian Pulp and Paper, etc., and at that dinner he raised $700,000 to cover the expenses for the Conference. As participants we had to pay our own travel expenses to get there and home, but apart from that everything was paid for. On the last day we had some time off in Vancouver and we got on a bus and were quite affronted when they asked us to pay! We had not been accustomed to paying when we got on and off coaches, and we were always treated with proper dignity. In Toronto at Edwards Gardens (Toronto Botanical Garden) we were travelling in a column of coaches and we came out of there in downtown Toronto at about five o'clock in the evening, we had our escort (which we were accustomed to) and they rode out into the middle of the highway at rush hour and stopped all traffic. We sailed through.

We travelled by train from Montreal to Ottawa and that's where we learned about the permafrost. The ride was very rough and it was explained to us that the ground never really thawed out. We had lectures all day in a big auditorium, and we had lunch there, then a group of us who were farmers met with the Canadian Minister of Agriculture. People with different interests met with various dignitaries. That evening we went to Rideau Hall (Governor General Georges Vanier's residence) for a reception. In our group we had one Indian fellow named Mr. Mohadev Singh, who was a dyed-in-the-wool anti-monarchist, so we all decided to keep him far away from Philip. At Rideau Hall we came in a side door and we had to go down a staircase and around a corner, so we were doing this in a dignified way when we heard a commotion and I said, "Lord, Singh has probably attacked the Prince!" When we got to the corridor we found out it was a fellow from Ghana who prostrated himself before the Prince (nothing worse than that). Anyhow we had a nice reception there then we travelled back to Montreal by train.

The opening ceremonies were held at the Université de Montréal and Prince Philip officially opened the new men's residence while we were staying there. They held a ceremony and invited some people to lunch where I met a fellow I kept in touch with for years. He had a wife and five or six children and he worked on the railroad. He was taking a night school course in the science of anaesthetising people by hypnosis, as opposed to artificial means. He was a conductor on a train and when he came home in the evening his wife would have a hot meal waiting for him, he would see a little of the children then go to the University from seven to ten o'clock, six days a week. It was a four-year course and he had been taking it for two years. I asked him how he found time to do anything else and he said every Sunday was devoted to the children. I was much impressed with him.

My group was fifteen strong; the leader of my group was Peter Allen, Senior Personnel Officer for Trans Canada Pipelines. One fellow was the senior personnel officer of Holden, the Australian division of General Motors. Singh was the head of a textile trade union in India, and I remember this very nice fellow who was chairman of the civil service commission in New Zealand. There were two English fellows; one was chairman of an oil company in Leeds, the other one was secretary of the electrical workers' trade union in the shipbuilding business in Sunderland. One fellow was from Africa, and there was Angie from Malaysia (the only one I have continued to keep in touch with). Basically, there were trade unionists, civil servants, and managers in each study group, reflecting a diversity of the whole membership; 40% of the members from corporate management, 40% from trade unions and 20% from public administration or the volunteer sector.

Peter explained to us that each study group had to present its individual report of impressions and observations made during the twenty-four-day trip right across the country (and he said he wasn't having any minority report from group H). Every evening when we got back to our accommodations we would meet and thrash out a unanimous report. For instance, when we went to the gold mine, some people spoke to mine managers, while others spoke to the miners down below. We had different experiences to share with each other and we had to find a consensus before Peter would let us go to bed. At six o'clock the next morning there were papers under your door, detailing the day's schedule and activities. We had Pat Pickney as secretary to our group (a very nice girl, she was the secretary for the chairman of Seagram's). When we got to where we were going our luggage would be in our rooms, if you wanted any laundry done you gave it to Pat, if you wanted anything posted you gave it to Pat. She travelled with our group throughout the whole trip and following one particularly long and gruelling session, when we had arrived at a consensus, this African fellow said, "Well, I don't know about you but I'm going to fuck off to bed." Our mouths opened! The poor fellow had been hearing the Australians use the expression, but he had no idea what it meant. He was mortified when we told him, and we couldn't get him back into the clan after that, he was always off by himself and we couldn't persuade him to join us again. He was so ashamed because Pat was there.

Different groups were sent to different parts of Canada and it was made plain to us that we were not to examine Canadian industry; we were to examine the human effects of industrialisation on people. Our group was assigned to Northern Ontario; Kirkland Lake, Sudbury, (Noranda) Timmins (Pamour Porcupine). When we got to the airport there was a DC3 waiting for us with a Shell Oil insignia on the door. The chairman of Shell had lent us his corporation's private plane to fly us up to Timmins.

When we got to Timmins there was a big sign across the road saying, "Welcome to the Duke's Do." We had a reception with the Mayor and local dignitaries. Two fellows took two of us out to Timmins Golf Club, owned by the Hollinger Mine. It cost Cdn. $700 to join and another $700 per year in fees. A beautiful place with beautiful greens, we came back in after playing at around eleven o'clock in the evening–our hotel dining room was long since shut down, so they took us to a place looking for dinner and it was pretty damn cold by that time. When we left Toronto it was 76° F but then the temperature dropped as night fell and it got very cold. It was fairly warm when we landed in Timmins but going out with those fellows and staying out until midnight I caught a nasty cold. The next day we were invited to the Hollinger Mine manager's lodge. They had a beautiful smoked salmon but I was feeling horrible and all I could do was sit in a corner and look on. Various things stick in my mind, like the lake which was very close, maybe 100' away and one of the mangers told me that up until two weeks ago you couldn't see the lake, but the beavers had cut down all the trees!

We visited some of the gold mines in the area and I spent an hour and a half, 2 ½ miles down in this mine shaft and I was expected to walk around and talk to the miners. Most of the miners came from Central and Eastern Europe; from places like Bulgaria and Hungary, and before I went down I was told that there were two West Indians on the roster, but they couldn't be found. We had to be checked in and checked out–you couldn't just disappear in the mines–but they disappeared. West Indians, you know!

One of the other things that sticks in my mind is when we went to a highschool and the principal told us that the children of new immigrants were at the top of all his classes, their children (second generation immigrants) were in the middle of all his classes and the third generation were at the bottom.

All the conference members foregathered at the University of Toronto, where we had endless lectures again. Then we boarded two separate trains–half went by Canadian Pacific Railway (CPR) and half went Canadian National Railway (CNR). Our group travelled at night aboard CNR and the first evening we stopped in Hornpayne, Ontario to visit a dying boiler works. We spent an evening there with two couples who were trying not to leave, but their income had vanished.

Then we travelled all night and the next day we were in Winnipeg. We spent a lot of time at the University of Manitoba, we didn't see much of Winnipeg. Then we travelled all night and we were into Saskatoon. There we did some exciting things. They had invited homesteaders out there to come in and have lunch with us as guests of the Conference. And they served buffalo steaks. This couple (the Malickys) came and took an Englishman and myself out of town to their farm seventy miles away. They told us about their son Bob who was at college, and about all the chores he had to do when he came home. When we were getting there, they asked us, "What would you like to do most?" The Englishman said what he wanted most was a bed. I thought it wasn't very exciting for these people to come seventy miles to pick us up and drive all the way back, so I asked them if I might also take a bed but please wake me when Bob comes in. It was kind of sleeting and they lent me a tin hat and a pair of Wellingtons and I went out with Bob and brought in the cows, I helped him and watched him milk the cows and feed the calves, there were only four or five cows but he had to muck out the pig sty and feed the chickens and all sorts of things! The Malickys also had two daughters and we kept in touch for ages. Bob went through University and took over running the farm and the parents moved into Saskatoon.

We travelled all night and into Edmonton. When we were there a few of us were going to have tea with the Oil Wives (who were soon known as the Old Wives) and their children. In every case when the kids heard that I grew bananas I was the centre of attraction; I had to explain to them how bananas grow, how they are harvested, what you did with them and so on. There was a small town called Edson, about thirty miles west of Edmonton and they had recently celebrated their 50th anniversary as a town. One of the townsmen had written a play about the evolution of the town, which they had put on for their own enjoyment and pretty much the whole town came in to watch them present it to us at the University of Alberta in Edmonton. They said we were such an appreciative audience that they got better and better as they went along. We spent two days there and we all had a great time. Another conference member and I had lunch with a man and a woman who were real old-timers there. She said her husband was a trapper and a prospector and she lived out there, but she was the only white woman around so she was expected to lay on dinner for them every Saturday night. She said that in the winter time she had to dress up the baby and go about a quarter of a mile through the snow just to get a bucket of water. Then some fool like me said, "Why don't you melt the snow?"

"Snow!" she said, "Do you realise how much snow you would have to melt to get a bucket of water? It would fill up this whole room!"

This trapper/prospector had made three gold strikes. Each time he made a gold strike he would come down and register it and then he sold it out to some company and went on a glorious spree and when he woke up he was broke. Three times! Once when he was out prospecting, he came back to find a wolf nosing in his pack and he threw his hammer at it and the wolf took off. When he went to pick up his hammer he saw a glint, and it was gold. That was his second strike. I suppose that's happened a hundred, or maybe a thousand times. Anyway it was interesting meeting those people from Edson. During one of these visits somebody came flying in on a motorcycle, asking for the keys to the Post Office, saying the Post Office must be opened, and that the Post Master had gone off with the keys!

We spent two days there and on the second evening we took off by train, which was my undoing. Each of us had a roomette and there was a steward on this train who was from St. Lucia and had been in the agricultural industry. He came and told me the Australians were having a party in the front of the train and they wanted me to come. So I did. I was returning to my roomette in the early morning when we saw the sun glinting off the peaks of the Rocky Mountains. It was so beautiful that we went into the caboose at the back of the train and drank some more whiskey. By the time we got to Banff I had a terrible headache and I missed going to see the glacier, which I've always regretted. We spent the day there and the next day it was down into British Columbia. We passed near Mount Robson, the highest point in the Canadian Rockies.

All this time Philip had been on a ranch in Alberta and he joined us at UBC (University of British Columbia). When it came to presenting our report, our group decided that I should do it. I was trembling like a leaf. I had to go up on stage and Prince Philip was sitting at a desk and I had to stand up near to him and read this report.

On one of our expeditions up in Northern Ontario I had spent a Sunday with a mine manager who was going to take me trout fishing. He lived on a lake and he had a boat, but it rained, and there again the kids wanted to know about bananas. It was illegal to take ore from the mine but the sons of the mine manager dug a ditch across the road where the trucks (loaded with ore) would drive by on their way to the smelter. When the trucks drove over this ditch, ore would bounce off the truck, and I had one of these pieces of ore in my hand when I went up on stage to give our group's report.

When I had finished and was leaving the stage I remembered that I had left the rock on the desk beside the Prince. I turned around to retrieve it but he swept it up and put it into his pocket. It may be a paperweight on his desk now but I don't have it anymore.

Delivering our group's report at UBC

Grenville Harbour

Tawana

Whilst at Dennery, we had a visit from Major Ray Thompson, L. Rose & Company's man in Dominica. They wanted to contract with Dennery to grow limes to supply them. I told him that Craigston could supply lime juice right away from Carriacou. I contacted my brother Paul in Grenada, who was running the Carriacou business, and it was agreed that Ray Thompson should meet Paul and I in Grenada and go to Carriacou together so that Ray could see the plantation and machinery, and get an idea of the product.

When I got to Grenada, I found to my consternation that we were to embark on a yacht, *Tawana*, that my cousin Gordon Gentle had bought from Denis' older brother Bertie Barnard of St. Vincent. The gear box of this boat had been in a repair shop for some weeks before and had only been reinstalled the previous day. When I heard that there had not been any sea trials and we were setting out for Carriacou untested, with a large crew, it didn't seem to make sense. However, it was too late to make any change of plans so Paul and I, along with my cousin Gordon and two teenage lads; Steven Mascoll and Robbie Bains, were joined by Harry Brassington (representative of Farrows of Spalding, for whom Paul was agent) and Ray Thompson, who came straight from the airport to the boat.

We set out from the Grenville jetty at about 2:15 pm with Paul at the tiller, who guided us through the reef before handing over the helm to Gordon. We motored along the east coast of Grenada and the boat was rolling a bit–it wasn't rough but there was a bit of a swell–so Gordon decided to up sail. He sent Robbie and Steve forward to put up the jib as we rounded Telescope Point, but the main halyard jammed and the mainsail would not go up. I offered to help and went below to change into a bathing suit, then clambered forward but we were still unable to get it moving. The boat was rolling in a bit of a cross sea, so I suggested to Gordon that we run up under Sandy Island where we could sort it out.

We passed about half-a-mile to the east of Pearls Rock and I was gazing up at the mast in an effort to trace the paths of the various ropes. It was a gaff-rigged sloop and I'd never seen so much rope in my life! I looked to windward and was shocked to see an enormous wave bearing down on us. It had not broken but was white-capped and menacing and I exclaimed, "Gosh, I would run!" Gordon didn't know what I was talking about, then he saw it, and I think he was petrified. We held our course and the wave got nearer and nearer and higher and higher. I was hoping to see *Tawana* rise to it, but as it came alongside, I could see that it was about to break and there wasn't a thing to do but hold on and pray and I did both.

The wave appeared to be about twelve feet high as it reared up over our heads and smacked down on us like the cracking of a whip. I crossed my arms over my head and tried to avoid the boom and felt myself being hurled out of the cockpit into the water head first. At first I didn't know which way was up, but as the white water cleared and the roaring in my ears subsided, I straightened out and realised that debris all around me was floating to the top; all sorts of things like oranges, bottles of whiskey and bottles of rum, but I was being dragged down by a rope wrapped around my knees. I jack-knifed and followed the rope down, slackening it enough to be able to pull out one leg, then kicked the other free and I made for the surface. My lungs were bursting when I did break water. After a couple of deep breaths I shouted, "Where's everybody?"

Robbie pointed out that Gordon, Ray and Paul were behind me and Steven and Braff were quite near, so we were seven and all safe for the moment. As the boat went down and disappeared from sight, I looked for a bit of wreckage to hold onto. I saw the broken spar and started swimming toward it, then the plywood dingy that had been lashed to the deck came up among us. We all made for it and although it had been staved in and was full of water, it had enough buoyancy to help us. Paul had clambered onto a hatch cover and we decided to keep together and head for the nearest land which was Conference Beach.

We hung onto the dinghy with one hand and kicked and paddled with our free hands. The sea was moderately rough but few waves were breaking and didn't cover us. None of us had any idea which way the tide was running, so I took a mark on Pearls Rock and Telescope Point and determined with relief that the tide was carrying us toward the shore. By watching coconut trees and various things on the mainland, we knew that the current was taking us up the coast toward Levera and that if we only persevered, eventually we would hit shore. It was about this time that Ray said, "I'll never make it."

And I said, "Don't be so stupid Ray. Either we're all going to make it or none of us will make it. If we stick together, we'll all make it."

We held onto the plywood dinghy and continued paddling. Every now and then as we put more pressure on this poor dinghy it would go lower and lower in the water, and in the midst of all this tension, Harry Brassington, who was a perpetual joker said, "I've got a fag, anybody got a match?" So we all laughed of course, which broke the tension.

With waves breaking to the north and south of us, we went into the channel and amazingly got past the reef and headed slowly for the shore; not fighting the current, but making use of it. As we got closer to shore we could see three figures standing on a little headland between Pearls and Conference beaches looking at us and Ray said, "Oh I won't be able to go ashore!"

And I said, "Why on earth can't you go ashore?"

"I don't have any clothes on!" he said. He had stepped off the plane and aboard Tawana fully clothed, but his trousers and shoes and socks and shirt and watch, everything but his vest, had been stripped off and lost.

And Gordon said, "Ray if we get ashore I couldn't care less what you have or what you don't have!"

As we got closer to shore we could see the surf pounding on the rocks off that point, so we decided to ease over to the north and try to land on the beach. When we were about a hundred yards from the beach, Steve and Robbie swam on ahead and were able to help Paul who got rolled up onto the beach with the hatch cover and was pretty badly winded. He said that if those two lads had not come to rescue him he would have drowned right there. He did not have the energy to pull himself out of the water.

The rest of us stayed with that dinghy until it was snatched from our grasp, then we helped each other ashore and then we were like a bunch of kids hugging each other, and wringing each other's hands, congratulating each other and thanking God for our delivery, saying, "Made it boys, we made it. We're all here!"

While there must have been about a hundred spectators on the beach when we came ashore, mostly women and children, none of them got their feet wet. They told us that at least one boat every year got overwhelmed by this wave, or its brother, and this puzzled us. One of them had run to the nearest telephone and called the Grenville Police Station. We learned that they were just preparing a schooner to come to look for us, but luckily we could tell them that we were already ashore.

Somebody had called Jean in St. Lucia to say there was a yacht sunk off the east coast of Grenada. She was all in a tizzy when somebody else called to tell her the same thing, but said that all the crew had been saved. So that was a relief. One chap appeared with a Land Rover and kindly took us up to Paul's where we celebrated our delivery. It was quite a celebration, as you can imagine.

The next morning I kept the vow I made and went to church. Then Harry and I went down to Conference Beach to see what there was left of the boat and saw bits and pieces of the hull strewn all along the coast. The gearbox can't be blamed, although it had been the cause of my apprehension. We could see that she had been pretty rotten and considered ourselves lucky that it had happened where it did. That was the end of *Tawana.*

Later we examined the chart of the area and saw this neck of underwater land; the floor was thirteen fathoms deep and the top was at eight fathoms, and we could only presume that the Atlantic surge coming in would build up until one enormous wave would develop. *Tawana* went down in about twelve fathoms, about a mile and a half from the shore.

Paul, who was a bit delicate, spent six weeks in bed with pneumonia after that episode. Paul had always been a bit delicate, the tale goes that he drank a bottle of brandy before he was six weeks old. This was out in the country and the GP told Mother, "Louie, give the kid a teaspoonful of brandy in his bottle, it will do him a world of good."

I think that for the first six weeks they didn't think he would live, but he did, he pulled through.

Ray never did get to Carriacou. He went back to Dominica and sometime later he went to England. He had a haematoma on his back as a result of the shipwreck and they removed quite a lot of blood. He must have taken a blow somewhere in the mêlée.

And in spite of our shipwrecked expedition, Rose's contracted Craigston to supply lime juice, *Tawana* notwithstanding.

Cadbury Schweppes Limited

1-10 CONNAUGHT PLACE LONDON W2 2EX TELEPHONE 01-262 1212 TELEGRAMS CASCH LONDON W2 2EX

FROM THE CHAIRMAN G.A.H. CADBURY

9th June 1977

Dear Mr. Kent,

Thank you for your letter of 19th May and I am sorry I was not able to get in touch with you while you were in England, due to the time it took your letter to reach me.

I should make it clear that the margins we earned on that part of our business, which includes lime juice, are 7½% of sales. This is barely adequate to provide us with the funds we need to re-invest back in the business, if we are to keep our plant and buildings up-to-date and remain competitive.

You are right in saying that the cocoa price has increased rapidly and is at present some four times what it was in 1976. Unfortunately the actual producers in the main cocoa growing country, Ghana, receive only a fraction of the world price. The Ghana Marketing Board, on behalf of the government, tax the difference between the world price and the price to the farmer and uses it to finance government projects.

I do indeed understand the problem you face at Carriacou but the fact is that the price today for limes in Dominica and the neighbouring islands is much higher than that paid anywhere else in the world. It is higher than the price paid in Mexico and around double the price paid in Ghana and Tanzania, on top of which there is the additional cost of freight in the case of Carriacou. We are, therefore, paying a high premium for Carriacou juice and have been prepared to do this to maintain a traditional source of supply, although we could have met our requirements at lower costs elsewhere.

I will, of course, ensure that your letter is seen by the Managing Director and by the head of our Concentrates and Essences Division who is, naturally, thoroughly familiar with the situation in Dominica.

Thank you for writing and for putting the choices before you so clearly.

Yours sincerely,

E. R. Kent, Esq.,
Craigston Estate,
Carriacou, Grenada,
West Indies.

1970; Craigston shipped 70,000 gallons of lime juice to Rose's, Dominica.

1971 to 1976; drought

1972; Craigston produced only 200 gallons of lime juice--cost prohibitive to ship, juice turned to vinegar and disposed of.

*dumped into the sea 2-barrels at a time, to reduce environmental impact

St. Lucia
Model Farms

In 1980 I received a telegram from John Hailwood (CEO Geest, St. Lucia) asking if he and Frankie Leonce could fly down to Carriacou to discuss a proposition with me. I agreed and they flew down a few days later.

John Hailwood explained that Geest wanted desperately to be rid of their St. Lucia estates as they were losing money at a prodigious rate. He explained that, to shut them down would create a lot of unemployment and cause some social upheaval. Geest, in collaboration with Commonwealth Development Corporation and The Government of St. Lucia had agreed to sponsor the St. Lucia Model Farms Project, the object of which was to split Roseau Estate into 5-acre banana farms on the 1,000 acres of flat lands, and 10-acre farms of diversified crops on the 600-acre hillside.

I was asked to launch the project as Project Manager. I realised that my primary role would be to train the previous Roseau Estate farm workers to become farm managers, as they were to be given a great deal of autonomy from the day the farms were handed over to them, and until they had finished paying for the farms, at which time they would own them outright.

I consented to visit Roseau before deciding, and did so. I was visited whilst there by Dr. John Sessing, a Jamaican with a PhD in agricultural engineering. He had been employed there for two years as technical director and urged me to join him in launching this project. I had a very high regard for him and I was sorely tempted. However, after further consideration I realised how many people's employment was dependant upon me on Carriacou and I declined the offer.

A year later, with the Communist PRG (People's Revolutionary Government) more entrenched in Grenada and Carriacou, I reconsidered and enquired of John Hailwood if the vacancy still existed. It did, and the offer was renewed, so reluctantly leaving my employees to their own fate, my wife and I moved to St. Lucia in November 1981.

I looked forward to cooperating with Dr. John Sessing to get the project launched and as I mentioned before, I had a very high regard for him and liked him very much. When I decided to return to St. Lucia what appealed to me was that I was to train farm workers to become farm managers. Nobody believed it would succeed and nobody wanted to go and work there, and everybody smirked when you spoke about St. Lucia Model Farms.

Jean and I were accommodated in a rented house on the Vigie Peninsula and an ancient Land Rover, which had probably served many managers before me, was placed at my disposal. A few days after I arrived, it was agreed with Hailwood, that I should assume duties as manager of Geest's Roseau Estate, as it had not yet become a joint project and it had not yet been transferred to SLMF. Indeed, a political impasse had arisen, the Louisy government had fallen, and an interim government had been appointed until general elections could be held. It was felt that this interim administration could not sign the respective guarantees for the (XCD $2 million) seed money that each of the partners, (Government of St. Lucia, CDC and Geest) were obliged to put into the project. So, much to my chagrin, I was asked to manage Roseau for Geest until these matters could be settled. Thus, when I went to take over, I expected that Hailwood as chairman of Geest Estates Ltd., would come to "hand over" to me. When he did not appear, Dr. Sessing called him and was told, "No! I'm not coming, let Edward take over!"

This was not a very auspicious beginning as I had to take charge of some 1,600 acres with 168 workers and a staff of 16, with assorted vehicles; trucks, tractors, Land Rovers and lesser rolling stock. I knew almost none of the workers or staff, so it was a good thing that Dr. Sessing was there to introduce me.

I was advised that Geest had lost XCD $1.7 million running Roseau and Cul de Sac in the preceding fiscal year. It did not take an economist to understand that since Geest was paying out $23,000 to $25,000 per week through the pay windows while only shipping 800 or 900 boxes of bananas per week, and when the administrative costs were taken into consideration the $1.7 million loss became believable. The warehouses were filled with all the fertilisers, herbicides, fungicides and insecticides needed to put the cultivation into good production, but they were not being used to advantage.

Shortly after I assumed management there was a windblow that caused 6 to 7% loss at Marquis and Dennery, but 18% loss at Roseau.

Those early days were nervous days as I found the estate in a shocking condition. The banana fields were growing high in guinea grass and other weeds. Banana "trees" that had been harvested had not been cut down, drains had not been cleaned in years and what little cultivation there was, was riddled with leaf spot. The labour force was largely undisciplined and the estate was drifting along like a ship without captain or rudder. I stopped further application of fertilisers, and concentrated efforts on weed, nematode and borer control. The simplest operations like pruning, bunch cleaning and sleeving had to be taught.

In some ways it was a blessing that there was this unexpected interim period because it gave me twelve months to determine which members of staff were pulling their weight. I was blessed to have Dr. John Sessing, the accountant Ashby Joseph, Mr. Mathew, and my secretary Ms. Flood to "guard the gate" with me. Though work was supposed to start at 7:30 a.m., I had observed on a previous assignment for Hailwood that hardly anything moved at Roseau before 8:30 or 9:00 a.m. At 10:30 a.m. workers were still waiting on the roadsides for fertiliser or nematocide, or other inputs to be delivered. Workers were given a fixed amount of bags to apply and as a result, the workers often carried it to the back of the fields and dumped it in the ravines. When Dr. Sessing started ploughing for new farms, the tractors dug up bags and bags of expensive nematocide that had never been opened. Tray-loads of fertiliser were similarly dumped.

I started leaving home at 6:30 a.m. and was at my desk by 7:10 a.m. each morning. In a short while I would find the other staff members waiting for me. We would confer and by about 7:25 a.m. I'd say, "Right fellas, let's get this estate rolling!"

. . . and we did.

Somehow that first year passed. The political and financial matters were resolved and I was told that St. Lucia Model Farms would officially commence operations on 1st January, 1983. A board of directors comprising two members from each of the partners; government, Geest and CDC were appointed. The first chairman was Julian Hunte, but with the change of government he was replaced by Leslie Clarke. I was not a director, but as project manager, I attended all board meetings. At the last meeting prior to handover, I said that the workers' union would have to be notified. Hailwood said, "No! We have a non-agreement with the union!" I protested that we had no reason to believe that the union did not still represent the workers, but Hailwood was adamant and the other directors were silent. As the meeting broke up the two CDC directors said, "Don't worry Edward! We're behind you!"

"Behind me?" I protested. "I don't want you behind me. When the trouble breaks out you will be in your air-conditioned offices and I will be under the gun. I want you in front of me!" They saw how angry I was and said no more.

In the middle of December, Hailwood sent me some 200 forms of "dismissal from Geest's service," to be distributed to staff and workers alike. I was informed by Hailwood that I should re-employ whoever I wanted to retain for SLMF. To my amazement, I saw that provision had been made at the bottom of the forms to be signed by E.R. Kent. I rang Hailwood to protest: He said, "I'm off to England tomorrow for Christmas! No time to change them now!" I did not want to delay the birth of SLMF by one more day. I couldn't imagine Mr. Carasco, Frankie Leonce or Abel Ghirawoo signing the forms, so I signed them and had them distributed. We then had to decide who we would re-employ and ascertain their willingness to work for SLMF.

With the inception of SLMF on 1st January 1983, I found myself in charge of 1,600 acres of the former Roseau Estate (1,000 acres of flat land and 600 acres of hillside land on the northern slopes of the valley). I had a staff of fourteen, three Caterpillar tractors and a wheeled tractor, a JCB back-hoe, three trucks and three Land Rovers. I also had XCD $2 million in the bank and a chequebook. I was told that myself and any of the six directors could sign cheques.

It was evident that if we continued to run the estate as it had been run we would soon run out of funds. We retained 14 of the 16 staff, and approximately 140 of the 168 field workers. You can imagine the curses and angry shouts of, "You fire me!" that greeted me as I drove 'round the valley. I went around explaining to the workers that Geest no longer owned the estate and that funds were limited. I told them that if they went into the field and cleaned and saved just three bunches of bananas per day, I could give them or their relative another day's work.

I never did understand how, in the first nine months of SLMF we were able to turn that tremendous loss into a gross "working profit" of some $90,000. By adopting the strategy of being at my desk by 7:10 a.m. each working morning, we would organise the work and the transportation and by 7:30 a.m. they were on their way to their separate sections or departments. I bought a cutlass and spent a lot of time in the field teaching and encouraging.

No one had seen a manager carrying a cutlass before so I was asked if it was intended for my defense? I explained that when I went into a field and saw a leaf rubbing on a bunch of bananas I could just cut off the leaf and not have to remember to tell an overseer to send someone to do so. But maybe there was an element of truth in the assumption.

One day shortly after I joined, I was on a tour of exploration behind the factory. This was where the spent lees (sediment from fermentation of rum) from the distillery ran in an open drain to the sea. The area was black with the lees, there were three enormous clumps of bamboo and altogether the area was pretty dismal. I surprised an elderly man who started when he saw me and asked in an agitated way, "What you doing here? They have a lot of evil spirits here. You mustn't come here by yourself!"

With more self-assurance than I actually felt, I replied, "You know Ah come from Carriacou, and Carriacou is the home of science, plenty spirits! Ah just come to visit me friends!" The man took off at high speed. I have often wondered if this chance exchange gave me a reputation of having "evil spirits" at my command, and perhaps this protected me from harm.

I had already been given the unenviable task of dismissing all of Geest's workers and although I did re-employ more than half of them, I had to instil some discipline, and this did not go down well. I knew that the first working day of SLMF would be rough, as I had several tasks to immediately accomplish: 1) Re-employ staff and workers; 2) We had to harvest bananas; 3) I had to receive a high-level delegation comprising Egbert Tai, Louis Verteuil, and one other person who had arrived from Martinique at 7:00 a.m., and who were all experts in tree crop husbandry.

I did not anticipate finding all the former Geest workers in the yard at 7:10 a.m. on that first morning. I had to drive slowly through the crowd, park and go up to my office. The chief security officer, Mr. Polius, was barring the stairway but I told him to let the people up. They poured into my office. Fortunately I recognised the leader, Mrs. Michelle who had worked in Willie Rapier's office. I rose and greeted her warmly, pulled out a chair for her and said, "Mrs. Michelle, we couldn't possibly have any fruitful dialogue with all these people around. Would you mind asking them to wait downstairs?" To my relief she did. Only the four union officials remained and informed me that the union was demanding recognition. I replied that it was not within my terms of reference to grant the union recognition. I would go to Castries and convey the demand to Leslie Clarke, Chairman of the Board. Mercifully, they agreed to this. I sped to Castries and the chairman agreed to meet with the union representatives two days hence. I sped back to Roseau, Mrs. Michelle ordered the workers to work, the crowd dispersed without incident and the harvesting commenced. Two days later the chairman and I met with the union representatives. The chairman asked them to put their demands in writing. We left his office together and I never heard another peep from the union during my three-and-a-half years at SLMF.

But my troubles were just beginning. All Geest workers had to be severed before any were rehired. A large sum of money and lists of names were sent from head office in Castries. The newly employed SLMF staff paid off the workers according to the lists received, but early next morning my office and stairway were filled with ex-workers who were protesting that they had not received sufficient severance pay. I sat them down one by one, noted their objections, explained that I didn't even know the formula by which severance pay was calculated. When I had listed a dozen objections, I sped to Geest's Castries office. No one there seemed sure of the precise wording of the legislation that dictated the amounts to be paid. I suggested that Geest's attorney be consulted but I was told, "He wouldn't know." So I crossed to the government printery and purchased two copies of their pamphlet covering CONDITIONS OF EMPLOYMENT. I left one copy with head office and sped back to Roseau to explain to the ex-workers that head office was correcting "errors & omissions." Some workers accepted my explanation but some–especially those who had not been re-employed–were quite belligerent. I had to display a degree of calm that I did not feel inside, but eventually they accepted my assurance that the matter would be rectified the following day. Indeed, on Tuesday an amended list and more cash came from head office and we had another "payday." We had yet another one of these paydays the next day, so that by Thursday the workers were asking jokingly, "When is the next payday?"

By Thursday I wrote to Mr. Carasco explaining that I had been unable to attend to SLMF affairs for the week, so would he please send someone from head office to deal with the outstanding Geest business. Fortunately we had been able to defuse the situation, so this became unnecessary.

I discovered a remarkable system by which work started (or was supposed to start) at 7:30 a.m. There was a tea break from 9:00 to 9:20 a.m. and work was supposed to continue until noon, then resume at 12:30 p.m. until 3:30 p.m. I preached that it was ridiculous to expect the busy mothers to feed and get their children to school in the morning, besides feeding themselves and the rest of their family, then walk home at noon, feed the family and themselves in half-an-hour and be back by 12:30 p.m. When I felt confident enough, I abolished the tea-break and increased the lunch-break to an hour. I waited for the heavens to fall, but nothing adverse happened.

It was fortunate that Hailwood had authorized the preparation of Model Farms during the interim period while Geest was still paying the bills. John Sessing and I had started the subdivision with the help of the surveyor, Mr. Guard. We had even traced out a path for the road to be built to tap into the 600 acres of hillside land that SLMF had purchased.

It was while we were slogging up one of those hills that John told me that he had given notice of his resignation. I said, "What? Man, you're crazy! It's because of you I came." But he wanted to go back to Jamaica and grow flowers–anthuriums and lilies. He was tired of St. Lucia. I begged him to stay and although he withdrew his resignation, he only stayed for about a year, and then he left. But before he left he told me, "Ed, you'll never make it with these people. You'll have to import Chinese or Indians or somebody. I've been here with them three years and I can tell you, you'll never make it with them."

I did not see that "these people" were any worse than the people of the Mabouya Valley, with whom I had worked for 11 years at Dennery Factory Co. Ltd. When I first went to Dennery an old planter told me, "Those are the worst people in St. Lucia. As a young man I was sent there as a manager. I stayed 24 hours." I figured that if I had survived at Dennery I had reason to hope that I could make it at Roseau. Certainly I was not about to put my tail between my legs and run, but there were many anxious times and I only survived with God's help.

The whole concept of SLMF was new to the Caribbean, so problems had to be faced and solutions found as we went along. For example, part of the labor force was used to "husband" the old banana fields, while some had to be used for the planting and husbandry of the first five new farms. Since these selected farmers were not to be paid wages any longer, they could not be settled on their farms until after first harvest when they would have an income. They had families to support.

We started with five 5-acre farms and soon realised that the 1,600 acres we had acquired from Geest were mostly producing bananas of the Robusta variety but it was a board decision that the farms should be planted with Valerie. There was a small nursery growing the Valerie variety, which was bred by The United Fruit Co. and spirited out of Jamaica, so the Valerie nursery was expanded. There were also some scattered plants of Giant Cavendish also known as Grand Naine or "Big Dwarf." Valerie's virtue was that it outproduced Robusta, and the fingers were relatively straight so that the hands packed better, and there was less bruising in the boxes. Later, I determined by field trials that the Grand Naine outproduced both the Robusta and Valerie, and it withstood drought equally well.

In planting and husbandry we were guided by a booklet on banana cultivation put out by The Windward Island Banana Research Station (WINBAN). In times to come I would be asked, "To what do you attribute the extraordinary production at Model Farms?" I would produce this booklet and say, "This is our banana Bible. The only difference is that we follow it scrupulously and our neighbours don't."

The only variation to WINBAN's recommendations was that we put ¼ lb. urea (chief solid component of mammalian urine) at the bottom of each hole at planting. We figured that the new roots would be at the bottom of the hole and it would take a long time for fertiliser placed on the surface to filter down. It seemed to work, as our highest producing farmer sold 24 tons per acre in his first full year. Thirty farmers each sold more than 15 tons per acre. I emphasise that they sold that much, not to say produced. They had to sort and discard any fruit that was scarred or damaged in any way.

To put it into perspective, SLMF was located in a river valley, a thousand acres, completely flat with the river running through it. The Windward Island Banana Research Station was across the river, with the same soil and weather conditions, and they never sold more than 12 tons per acre. Even the big estates like Geest, with all their English and Dutch and French and West Indian managers, never sold more than 8 tons per acre. Now it's true we had to prepare the land and plant the bananas and we brought them up to first harvest, but nevertheless it showed what could be done.

Geest had given permission for the establishment of five farms during their year in control. We advertised for applicants and got about forty, but few of the workers understood how the scheme was to work. We hardly knew ourselves, and there was no one to guide us. With the help of our accountant, Ashby Joseph, we established a system by which SLMF purchased inputs (fertiliser, herbicide, nematocide, spray cans, etc.) in bulk and sold them to the farmers on a nonprofit basis. SLMF sold the farmers' fruit and kept individual accounts for each farmer. At the end of each quarter the surplus on the individual farmer's account was paid out to him, after debiting for his inputs and shed (constructed for sorting, handling and storage of bananas, boxes, tools, etc.). An administrative charge was deducted and an installment toward the purchase of the farm he was working. Fifteen farmers took home between XCD $40,000 and $50,000, another fifteen took home between $30,000 and $40,000 from their farms of approximately 5 acres. Our top producing farmer (24 tons) took home XCD $66,000 from 4.73 acres.

When I accepted the post, I insisted that the one activity in which I did not wish to participate was the selection of farmers to be settled. I stressed that this was a task in which St. Lucians should predominate. Inevitably the early screening of applicants was left to me and my staff. The first forty applicants were interviewed by us and reduced to some fifteen. Two directors–one from Geest, the other from government–and I selected the first five farmers to be settled.

In April of 1982 Prime Minister John Compton, along with a party of officials and invited guests came to Roseau to hand over the first five farms. There was a brief ceremony, the farms were handed over and they returned to Castries, never to be seen again at Roseau in my time.

I tried to explain their new role to the five new farmers. I said, "When you were a child your parents beat you to make you learn. Your teachers beat you to make you learn. When you go to university it is you who want to become a lawyer or a doctor, the professors don't care if you want to sleep all day or drink rum all night. Well, up until yesterday I wanted to know when you came to work and when you left and what you were doing. Tomorrow you're a university student. I don't want to know when you come or when you go, I only want to know that your farm is in good order."

Up to the time when we had settled twenty-three farmers I inspected their farms and showed them how to prune, apply herbicide, clean fruit, etc. After that, we recruited Mr. Willius–a recent graduate from UWI–who took on that role. It became his responsibility to inspect every farm at least once per week. The eight main functions to be performed on the farm (i.e., draining, propping, deflowering, sleeving, etc.) were recorded in a book that stayed on my desk. As he inspected, Mr. Willius would enter his observations and a grade from 1 to 5 (1 = poor/unacceptable; 5 = excellent) for each operation. Whenever I had a spare hour, I would look through the book and select the worst four or five farms and try to visit them myself. It worked.

Shortly after the first handover we were told that Lord Kindersley, Chairman of CDC, was to visit. One of the five selected farmers had an addiction to rum, which we were not aware of when he was selected. His was the first of the five farms to be seen as one approached from the public road. Unfortunately, his farm was in poor shape and my pleas to him fell on deaf ears. I could not order him to clean up his farm, I'd been stressing the autonomy they were to have. So I just told him that this Lord Kindersley was the man who had given a lot of money for SLMF, and if he was pleased with what he saw he might give some more to develop more farms. Two days before Lord Kindersley's visit, I took my cutlass and went to this farm (perhaps illegally) and started cutting down old trees and cleaning trash, etc. I was pleasantly surprised when the other four farmers joined me, and in no time we had the farm looking pretty good.

Quite early, the European Union had agreed to inject XCD $3.5 million for the development of the 600 acres of hillside into 10-acre farms with a base crop of bananas, but each farm was to have 4 acres of Graham mango and 1 acre of Tahiti lime trees inter-planted. The chances of getting these plants from the St. Lucia Ministry of Agriculture were slim, so we established a nursery around the boxing plant and produced our own. For the lime trees, this necessitated getting budwood (shoot of a plant bearing buds suitable for bud grafting) from the IFAC station in Martinique.

By this time John Sessing had been replaced as technical director by Lennard Leonce, who had a master's degree in agricultural engineering from McGill University in Canada. He did a splendid job of preparing the seventy-three farms that were to follow. Before he left for Jamaica, John Sessing had cut a road that gave access to the hillside farms and Lennard Leonce did a splendid job of terracing them. We established six farms with bananas, mangoes and limes, before I left in 1985.

All harvesting of fruit was done by the farmers, and each had his own individual shed. SLMF provided the boxes and collected the boxed fruit from the individual farms to be transported to the docks for shipment. As an incentive, Geest paid a bonus of three cents per pound if a farmer's shipment averaged more than 70% top quality fruit. We couldn't ask Geest to give us a report on each individual farmer so we grouped the farms into units of five and each farmer's boxes were stamped with his farm number. If any farmer's poor quality fruit caused the other four to lose their bonus he would be very unpopular with the others in his group. In addition, we did random checks at the boxing plant to ensure that good quality fruit was properly packed. The peer pressure worked and as a result our farmers regularly earned the bonus.

SLMF trucked the fruit to the buying depot where it was inspected by Geest's selectors. The selectors were in the habit of rejecting enough bananas to feed their families and friends, and I became very unpopular with them when I sent Mr. Scantlebury down to the docks on shipment days. I insisted that all fruit not purchased by Geest remained the property of the farmers and therefore must be returned to them. I had an argument with the selectors over this and explained to them, "Look man, we are only the custodians, those bananas belong to the farmer. We are only carrying them down and selling them for him. Up until the time that you accept them, those bananas belong to him."

Generally, relations between management and staff, and management and the farmers were good. My staff was loyal and supportive and helped me to weather many a storm.

There was one farmer named Mr. Louis who resisted authority. I went to his farm one day because his standard was falling. I was trying to explain something to him and show him how to prune bananas and he got rebellious and ordered me off his farm. Now I was faced with a dilemma. Here I'd been telling the farmers for weeks that they had autonomy. What do I do? So I put my nose in the air and I left his farm with as much dignity as I could summon. It wasn't many weeks before Mr. Louis asked me to come back. Okay, peace and love.

I used to meet with the farmers at least once a month to discuss any new matters and to field questions. On the occasion when I told them I would be leaving, Mr. Louis stood up and I wondered, Oh God, what's he going to say? "You always tell us you not too old to learn. We hope you could learn something from us."

"Yes," I said, "What is it?"

"You're a bit too hard," he said.

I had to think fast on my feet, so I said, "Well you know, if you're running a salt fish shop and you have a problem you could say, 'When I go home this evening I gonna ask me wife, or maybe when I have a drink with me friends.' Or you say, 'Maybe I'll decide that tomorrow.' But when you're running a company of this size, tomorrow has its own problems. So you have to make a decision, and make it now! And under the circumstances, sometimes you'll be right and sometimes you'll be wrong. Well, I apologize for the times when I was wrong." That satisfied him and he sat down.

The Board would meet in Castries, eight miles away, but they wouldn't come to Roseau, they were scared. There had been labour strikes down there before I joined. Shortly before I left, the chairman came down to speak to my farmers for the first time in all my years. (The Board used to resent me calling them my farmers, but I contended, "Yes, they're my farmers, I schooled them.") Having made his speech, the chairman asked if there were any questions or if anybody wanted to say anything, and Mr. Louis stood up. My heart sank right through to Australia!

"Mr. Kent has been a father to all of us," Mr. Louis said, and he sat down. It was touching and it still brings a tear to my eye when I think of it.

I told the farmers, "For the first time you have demonstrated that a farmer can stay on his/her farm and make more money than a bank clerk or civil servant in Castries."

We had a medical clinic at Roseau for the remaining estate workers and the farmers, and when the doctor came to collect his cheque, he was furious. He said, "These people are making more than professional men!"

I said, "Yes, Doc, but they work very hard, and they are professionals."

The bottom line was that men who used to take home $5,000 if they worked 50 weeks as farm workers, found themselves taking home unheard of wealth. When people heard about this scheme, doctors and lawyers and all kinds of people were saying, "Oh we want a farm!"

St. Lucia Prime Minister John Compton soon recognised the success of SLMF and he would send anybody of any importance visiting St. Lucia–Ambassador from China or Timbuktu–down to Model Farms to impress them. My staff said, "Mr. Kent, you'll have to get a public relations officer. All your time is being taken up showing people around." But we kept the project going and we had fun.

A good friend of mine named Lord Walston came out from England and bought a big estate in St. Lucia. He heard about the project and asked me to take him and show him around the Model Farms one morning when I was going to work. Lord Walston was staying in a hotel so I left home at half past six and passed by to pick him up. When we arrived, I gave him a chair and asked him to sit in the corner of the office while I discussed with my staff what needed to be done; who needed trucking, who needed banana plants moved, who needed fertiliser, whatever issues there were. Then at half past seven I said, "Okay fellas, let's get this estate moving." By quarter to eight everybody was out of the yard, so we worked very well as a team. When my assistants had left the office at half past seven, Lord Walston asked me, "Edward, do you do this every morning?" And I said, "Yes, Lord Walston, every morning." And he shook his head in disbelief.

The most encouragement I got was from an American professor who came to see this remarkable land settlement scheme. When he wrote his report about Roseau, he sent me a copy. The report stated, "The project manager is determined that the farmers will succeed, whether they want to or not."

It was a challenge, but for those years I did not socialise. Various people complained that they never saw me. I said, "I didn't come to St. Lucia to socialise, I came to St. Lucia to work." Everybody said this thing would fail but as the man said, I was determined.

I would come down to Carriacou about three times a year and spend a weekend. I would often go and see Prime Minister Blaize and tell him about Model Farms. He urged me to come and do the same thing in Grenada. I didn't really resign from SLMF, but when my contract came up, I didn't renew it. Foolishly perhaps–I was being paid (by the EU) XCD $7,500 per month, tax free. I had a house (with utilities paid) and a maid provided by the company. I had a brand new Honda Civic car for my domestic purposes and a brand-new Pajero 4x4 for my use on the estate.

When I was leaving St. Lucia, four years after having launched St. Lucia Model Farms, the chief security officer said, "Twenty-five years I been working on this estate. I see all kinda manager come and go–English, French, Scotch, even Dutch–but this is the first time I see a manager who cared about his workers."

Conducting VIP tour of St. Lucia Model Farms

St. Georges, Grenada

Grenada
Model Farms

In May of 1985 I returned to Carriacou and awaited a letter of appointment from the Honourable George Brizan, Minister of Agriculture. When by August I had received no word from him, I wrote telling him that I could not remain permanently unemployed, and I was seeking other employment. He hastily gave me a one-year contract as project manager of the new Grenada Model Farms.

When I went to Grenada in September, I found that I was not at all welcome. All I could hear in the Ministry of Agriculture was, "We do not want a carbon copy of St. Lucia Model Farms. We must do our own thing." I was given a large office with a large desk and a secretary who could hardly type a letter. I tried to find out as much as I could of the 23 government-owned estates, but eventually told the Minister, "Sir, we talk of Grenada Model Farms on the road, path, stairs, verandah, but we haven't sat down to talk about Model Farms." He hastily summoned a meeting with U.S. Aid and I told them that I didn't quite know what the object was–U.S. Aid was interested in privatizing the farms and I thought government was interested in getting rid of them–but my goal was to increase production on the farms. Which of these were we to pursue? I got no clear-cut answer but a few days later, the Minister announced in a meeting of the heads of divisions within the Ministry of Agriculture, that he wanted *Eddie* to take charge of all the Grenada farms. This was a tall order and not at all what I had gone to Grenada to try to accomplish. Nevertheless, I determined to do what I could in the short time allotted to me.

I soon found out that shortly after the intervention in 1983, wages on public works projects had been increased from XCD $12 to $16 per day (for men), but the wage for agricultural workers remained at $12. Understandably, 90% of the agricultural workers had gone to work on the road projects. One estate with cocoa, nutmeg, citrus, cloves, pimento and bananas was left with one elderly man and two elderly ladies. They could barely harvest the nutmegs and some of the cocoa, and the other crops remained unharvested.

I explained this situation to the Minister of Agriculture and to the Prime Minister, but neither seemed particularly interested. I realised that I would not be able to rock the boat, so I resolved to serve out my time quietly. Fortunately, the Minister had only given me a one-year contract, so I declined to renew it and in September of '86 I left the employment of the Ministry of Agriculture and returned to Carriacou at the end of the year.

Real Estate

Development on Carriacou

Whilst I had been living on St. Lucia, the harvesting and processing of limes had ceased on Carriacou, and there was no incentive to resume it. During my absence, my brother Paul had a 45-acre section of Craigston Estate subdivided for sale, by way of a housing development. Paul died on February 17, 1985. I had the plans, but no start had been made. Thus, with no training or direction, I turned my attention to real estate development. I labouriously searched out the markers laid down by the surveyor some years before.

I purchased a Bobcat (compact excavator) to continue with the road development. The Bobcat was landed at the end of the jetty and no one had the slightest idea how to drive it. Tony Joseph worked it out and drove it up to Craigston.

It was working at Harvey Vale and Tony said he heard "noise." He checked and found the noise coming from the rear end was the result of a broken gear. I complained to the Bobcat Agency, Plantrack in Barbados, who put me onto the manufacturer in Chicago. Plantrack sent a mechanic down to Carriacou, and he agreed that a gear had been stripped. Chicago would not send a gear–they sent a whole new gearbox which Tony and the mechanic from Barbados installed. Not long after, we had the same problem and Chicago told me that they had subcontracted with a foundry which had produced 75 of these gears which were sold to Bobcat, without being case hardened. I had got two!

At this stage, Bobcat in Chicago asked me to return the tractor to them. I had only to get it to St. Vincent . . . onboard a vessel with sheep and cows.

I spent $19,000 on that tractor, and attempts to recoup the money proved to be useless when we let it out to Gairy's man Charles Cayenne, who wanted to clean a pond. He was surprised when we billed him $50.

Further talks went on between Barbados, Chicago and also Peter Lang, who was the agent for Bobcat in St. Lucia. Eventually I was persuaded to buy a JCB (excavator) which came and gave sterling service until it was sold in the late 90s. That JCB cut all the Cherry Hill roads with Tony as the driver. It was also hired out to people digging footings and water tanks.

In early days, a number of Carriacouans applied to me for land to build a house but the prices for Snow Hill lots were beyond their means, so I was determined to do Cherry Hill development at more moderate prices.

In the 60s, Paul sold land to Curtis Knight at $1,000 an acre; so if I sold at 50¢ per square foot, it would be $21,780 an acre, so we proceeded to get a survey done of the Cherry Hill area and got development permission. Roads were cut, electricity was installed and lots were put on the market.

It soon became apparent that Carriacouans wished to live near the public road, whereas ex-pats preferred to live inside, far from the public road. It was a hard and tedious business, building concrete strips which served the development, but with the aid of two Land Rovers, two trailers and some trusty workmen, we got the job done.

I'm a Farmer, Your Majesty!

In 1992 I received a letter from the Governor General's office, inquiring delicately if I would be willing to accept an award from Her Majesty the Queen. It was all very hush hush and confidential. I wrote a reply to say I would accept it and the next thing I knew it was announced on the Queen's Birthday Honours that I had been awarded CBE.

Down at the bottom of the ladder you have MBE, (Member of the Order of the British Empire) then you have OBE (Office of the Order of the British Empire) then CBE (Commander of the Order of the British Empire) and KBE and GBE–that's knighthood. And I thought I might get an OBE, but I never thought I would get a CBE.

I had a choice of receiving the award from the Governor General here, or going to Buckingham Palace to be presented by The Queen. Well, I wasn't going to miss the chance to go to Buck' Palace!

Jean wouldn't go with me. . . so I left her here on Carriacou and I went with my daughter Diana and her husband David Wright, who live in England, and we had a lovely day. We were sent some directions as to when we were to present ourselves and they sent a sticker for our car. The cars were stopped outside the palace and thoroughly searched. Whenever I saw the Queen drive through in her carriage on TV, I always wondered where they went. Well there's a big courtyard in there and we drove into this courtyard.

We went into Buckingham Palace itself and up this beautiful staircase, where a gentleman at the bottom was taking away all cameras. I was separated from my guests–Diana and David went one way, and I went another, up into a big, beautifully decorated ballroom. There was a humourous fellow trying to put everybody at ease, then an equerry came around pinning something on all the other men. When he was finished, I said, "I did not get one of those."

And he said, "Yours goes 'round the neck, sir."

We were on the right side of this hall with a throne up at the front and we were led around into this antechamber where we all lined up and came out individually. The Queen was sitting about ten paces back so we were told to come out and walk (smartly) until we were opposite Her Majesty, do a sharp left turn, then approach Her. Then we were to shake her hand briefly.

While we were lined up waiting, I got talking to a pilot from New Zealand, and he was talking over me to a great big fellow, and when the other fellow went through I asked the pilot, "Who's that?" And

I can't remember his name, but he was a well-known cinema star, like Errol Flynn or somebody. My grandchildren were horrified to hear that I was standing right there next to him [Michael Caine] and didn't recognize him, because I had not been to the cinema much.

When it was my turn, I tried not to trip up or fall down or faint or anything. Then my name was called out, "Mr. Edward Kent, CBE." So I marched across, stopped, did a left turn, went up and Her Majesty said, "Oh Mr. Kent, what do you do?"

And I said, "I'm a farmer, Your Majesty." Then I thought quickly, that's pretty broad. . . so I said, "I grow bananas."

"Oh," she said. "But isn't that market in some jeopardy?"

At that stage the Windward Islands had some preferential treatment, freedom from taxes and so on, and the European Union and the Americans were trying to get this subsidy removed.

I said, "Yes your Majesty. But we are depending upon Her Majesty's government to protect it for us." That seemed to please her, and she smiled and asked me a couple more questions. Then she shook my hand and gave me a little push. That's it. It all happened in a flash.

You don't turn your back on Her Majesty when you exit, but I had gone perhaps two thirds of the way and started to turn, and then I realised I was not in place, so I hastily had to turn back and go four more paces backwards before turning. Then I went down into a room where the equerries were, and they immediately took my medal from me! They put it up nicely in a box.

Meanwhile, Diana and David were seated at the back with the other people in the audience, and when I came out they asked me, "What were you talking to the Queen about for so long?" I told them, and they said, "You were the longest talking to her!" Well, Her Majesty is very gracious. I met her several times, once in Government House in Grenada and once again in St. Lucia.

Epilogue

by Susan Payetta

Dr. Edward Roy Kent died on May 15, 2009. Two funerals were held on Wednesday, 20th of May. The morning service celebrating Edward's life filled Christ the King Anglican Church in Hillsborough on Carriacou to capacity. Heartfelt tributes told the tale of a lifetime filled with determination and commitment to work, family, history, and sport.

Later that afternoon a second and also very well-attended service was celebrated at St. Patrick's Anglican Church on Grenada, followed by interment at the church yard cemetery, where many Kent family members are buried. Edward was laid to rest here beside his beloved wife Jean.

While this collection of memoirs renders a sketch of Edward's long life and working career, it does not paint a complete picture of his life. These are the stories time permitted us to record. A devoted family man, Edward's wife Jean, their five children and many grandchildren were the focus of his everyday life.

In 2007 Edward had been bestowed with an honorary degree from The University of the West Indies, at St. Augustine Campus, Trinidad and Tobago. Although his area of expertise was in the field of agriculture, Edward always wanted to go to university to study law, and he accepted the Doctor of Laws *honoris causa* graciously. He treasured this honour, and was thrilled that he was asked to give the feature address at the ceremony. This he did with verve and charm in spite of his failing health. He invited many family members, friends and prominent citizens of Carriacou to share the occasion. He paid all expenses so that anyone who wanted to attend was given the opportunity. Edward enjoyed every minute of every activity on the graduation itinerary, cutting a stylish figure in the Trinidad Hilton's lobby, even as he got into the wheelchair his children insisted he use around the large spaces and long corridors of the hotel.

Edward's funeral service was another example of inclusion and his generosity. He had left instruction that round trip transportation was to be provided for those from Carriacou wishing to attend both services. The timing was tight, and when the bus chartered to take mourners from the ferry dock in St. George's to St. Patrick's pulled into the church yard directly behind the hearse at precisely 3:00 p.m., I knew Edward would have been the first to make a joke about nearly being late for his own funeral.

The gravediggers are actually burying the casket by hand. This is something I've never seen before. I come from another time and place than Edward does, where modern burials are done with machinery, and sometimes the ground is frozen so hard no one can be buried until spring thaw. Everything is more real and vivid here. The gravediggers are shoveling the earth fastidiously in rhythm with the hymns, with a unison common among manual labourers, taking turns, taking care to mound the earth in an exacting manner. I have never heard singing as lovely as today. If they could have, the choir would have high-fived each other when they hit that final high note, but it's a sombre occasion and they somehow manage to contain themselves. Everyone is quiet now, each of us concentrating on our own thoughts while the last few scattered stones, so recently displaced, are skilfully replaced with precision by the gravedigger who appears to be a perfectionist.

Onboard *Osprey* returning to Carriacou, we're passing Sauteurs, not far from where Edward has been laid to rest today. We're leaving the lee of Grenada and I'm thinking about those days when *Enterprise* hove-to off Tanga Langa Point to collect passengers bound for Carriacou. Edward told me the sea was always rough here, in fact that's how Tanga Langa got the name; rolling over big waves a ship's bell would ring as soon as she rounded the point. Ironically, the sea is as flat as glass this evening, a quiet time for reflection on a moonlit cruise through waters that are seldom calm. Recalling this conversation, it's here that I say goodbye to a dear friend.

THE UNIVERSITY OF THE WEST INDIES

Edward Kent

Chancellor,

Mr. Edward Kent combines remarkable talents for animal husbandry and crop production with business acumen and interpersonal skills.

Edward Kent is deeply grounded in the Caribbean through a Grenadian family traceable back to diverse roots – a British attorney and his Grenadian creole wife, who settled and became estate owners, as well as a privateer and his Carib wife whose descendents also established themselves as a farming family.

Prevented by World War II from fulfilling his dream of becoming a lawyer, Edward Kent journeyed to Carriacou to manage his father's property. Gradually, through his direction of various estates, he gained experience in agricultural management. Estates flourished under his care, his insight and gentle discipline setting him apart from other managers of his time, and his compassionate interventions and wise advice to workers entered into their own family sagas.

His crucial role as President of the Grenada Agriculturalist's Union in the recovery from Hurricane Janet (1955) brought wider attention to his work, and by 1957 he accepted the position of General Manager of the Dennery Factory in St Lucia. Here he guided the major transformation of this company, shifting from sugar to bananas. Then, as first Project Manager of St Lucia Model Farms, he settled and trained 778 farmers in the management and productive ownership of plots. On the invitation from the Prime Minister of Grenada to establish a similar scheme there, Edward Kent refused renewal of the contract in St Lucia and returned to Grenada - only to find lack of support in other areas of the government, resulting in inadequate funding for successful implementation.

Rallying from this bitter disappointment, he returned to Carriacou to build up the family estate. Here he has remained for the last twenty years, resuscitating and expanding the lime industry and, more importantly, experimenting brilliantly in cattle and sheep rearing through creative integration of experimental and traditional methods. From twelve pure bred Black Belly sheep from Barbados he produced a herd, shipping to St Lucia, St Vincent, Trinidad and Guyana and so upgrading livestock throughout the region. Similarly, importing pure bred bulls from Texas, Barbados and other areas he upgraded stock and bred tick free descendents. Driven out of lime oil and cocoa production by capitalist policies of low payment for Caribbean goods that have crippled farming regionally, Edward Kent nevertheless maintained his prize animals.

His reputation for success in breeding, together with his meticulous attention to records, has not only made him an important exporter but a resource for researchers on black belly sheep especially with regard to birthing records. Yet he is proficient not only in agricultural history but in the history and archeology of Carriacou and in his own family history, his incredible memory for events and names constituting a treasury of personal, popular and technical information. His substantial research and collection of artifacts and information have enhanced the Carriacou Historical Society and Museum, of which he is Historian.

Now retired from active farming, he has sold his estate but donated substantial land for local projects and he remains deeply valued as community member, grandfather and mentor. Well read, comfortable in academic circles despite having no formal degree, a model of old school courtesy and up to date communication skills, his friendships span seven decades extending to Malaysia and Australia and nurtured through his proficient employment of e-mail.

A multi-talented agriculturalist, estate manager, historian and philanthropist, Edward Kent has demonstrated a talent for life, a nurturing stewardship that has refined theory and practice in Caribbean farming and modeled mentorship.

Chancellor, I present Mr. Edward Kent and ask that by the authority vested in you by the Council and Senate of The University of the West Indies, you confer on him the degree of Doctor of Laws, honoris causa.

St. Augustine campus
Saturday 3rd November, 2007

www.ingramcontent.com/pod-product-compliance
Ingram Content Group UK Ltd.
Pitfield, Milton Keynes, MK11 3LW, UK
UKHW041829200726
13854UKWH00002BA/906